Gardner-Webb University
School of Divinity

This book donated
by

REV. C. O. GREENE

WHY THE CROSS?

WHY
THE CROSS?

G. RAY JORDAN

ABINGDON - COKESBURY PRESS

NEW YORK ● NASHVILLE

WHY THE CROSS?
Copyright, MCMXLI
By WHITMORE & STONE

Printed in the United States of America

To
RAY, JUNIOR
AND
TERRELL
WHOSE LIVES, I PRAY,
MAY ALWAYS BE GUIDED BY
AND DEDICATED TO
THE CHRIST OF THE CROSS

PREFACE

WHY THE CROSS? FOR CENTURIES THIS QUESTION HAS
provoked lengthy discussion—even heated dispute.
The theological implications, however, have too con-
sistently kept the discussion in the area of academic
argument.

Certainly there is deep mystery about the Cross. It
will likely never be fully understood. Those who do
grasp a bit of its truth must come to Golgotha in the
spirit of humility. Let no one approach Calvary—in-
tellectually or spiritually—save in the attitude of genuine reverence!

The Cross, however, is not merely mysterious; it is
intensely personal and gloriously challenging. It will
not let us go. Indeed, every Christian must face the
Cross for himself. It is with this more practical issue
presented by the Cross that the writer is concerned.
If the Cross has held such a vital place in Christianity
for nineteen hundred years, there must be some message it can speak to every honest soul.

Above everything else, the writer hopes that those
who read the pages that follow will seek to hear the
call of the Christ, as he challenges us with his thrilling
dare: "If any man will be my disciple, let him take up
his cross and follow me."

G. R. J.

CONTENTS

WHY THE CROSS?

WHY THE CROSS?

WHY THE CROSS, FOR JESUS?

From that time forth began Jesus to shew unto his disciples, how that he must go unto Jerusalem, and suffer many things of the elders and chief priests and scribes, and be killed, and be raised again the third day.

—MATTHEW 16:21

IT IS ALMOST IMPOSSIBLE TO OVEREMPHASIZE THE IMportance of the Cross. It is at the very heart of our religion. It presents an issue with which every Christian must deal. It is not a mere academic or theological question; it has to do with life itself. The more one studies it, the greater it grows.

In his old age, Tintoretto, the famous Venetian painter, asked to be taken once again to the seaside. He wanted to look upon the Adriatic another time. As his vision swept over the rolling waves, he exclaimed: "The sea always grows greater."

It is that way with the Cross. Its deeper meaning grows on us all the time.

There is something about the Cross so gripping, so sweeping in its power, that the longer one studies it, the more often one kneels before it, the more earnestly one ponders its significance, the larger it looms on the horizon of the mind. There is a reason for this. It is not simply because of the Cross. It is essentially because of that Strange Man who hung upon the Cross.

I

What were the experiences which brought him to Calvary? Why the Cross for Jesus, anyway?

Surely, there must be some explanation as to why Jesus felt that the Cross was inescapable. Apparently he could not avoid it. In those last days of his life, he kept saying things which clearly indicated that he must go to the Cross. He felt that it was inevitable.

"Ye know that after two days is the feast of the Passover, and the Son of man is betrayed to be crucified."

"Verily, verily, I say unto you, Except a corn of wheat fall into the ground and die, it abideth alone: but if it die, it bringeth forth much fruit."

"Verily I say unto you, that one of you shall betray me."

"From that time forth began Jesus to shew unto his disciples, how . . . . he must suffer . . . . and be killed."

The words move us deeply. We wish we could grasp their full meaning. But they seem to deal with something beyond our depth. If, however, first of all, we think of Jesus simply as a man in Galilee, who lived a life that led to a crucifixion, we may get hold of some truth that will help us more fully to appreciate this Strange Man.

II

Jesus could not escape the Cross because of *what* he was and because of *who* he was. There was not a chance for a man with the character of Jesus to avoid the Cross. He would not compromise with evil. He was not a coward. In one way or another, most of us seek to avoid difficulties. We want to escape them. Jesus did not want to suffer, either. He would have avoided the Cross if he could have done so without abandoning his sense of honor. That is the reason he prayed in the Garden of Gethsemane, "If it be possible, let this cup pass from me."

But it was not possible for the cup to pass because he refused to compromise with wrong or abandon his dreams and plans for the Kingdom of Heaven. He refused to alter either his purpose or his character.

If there had been a yellow streak in him, just one weakness in his soul, he might have escaped the Cross. We know how we are often afraid. We do not quite have the courage to suffer for right. It does not seem discreet to be uncompromising. At least, so we excuse ourselves. Jesus could not follow that course!

15

If he could have taken part of his courage out of his soul, and substituted for it a little bit of fear, and then explained to himself that the longer a man lives, the more work he is able to do, the better he can perform his service, the finer will be the character that he cultivates—he might have escaped.

If he had only been able to persuade himself that his duty and responsibility to his family necessitated his living, he might have avoided the Cross. If he could only have said to himself, "I owe it to my mother." Joseph was dead. It seems that the responsibility of supporting his mother had fallen upon him. That is why he turned to John and said, "Behold thy mother!" So, too, he said to Mary: "Woman, behold thy son!" Thus did he give the responsibility that he had borne to this intimate friend of his. Jesus, knowing that he was under obligation to his mother, and persuading himself that the longer he lived the finer service he might be able to render, could have said, "I owe it to my mother to avoid the Cross." Then he could have gone over into Transjordania and refused to face the crisis in Jerusalem. But Jesus was not a coward, not even enough of one to rationalize about his duty.

There were certain circumstances which inevitably forced the cross upon him. Jesus had to deal with men

16

whose hearts were filled with ill will, jealousy, malice, and hate. He was not responsible for these conditions. He had longed to save these people from all the forces that were warping their minds, from all the evil that was poisoning their hearts. But many of them would not listen to his warnings. He had not been able to change either them or the adverse circumstances. He had to confront a "religious" group who were determined to kill him, and a military government that his enemies could use in executing their plans.

Jesus faced the Cross because his loveliness was not desired by people who cared most for ugliness, because his character was not appreciated by people who were uninterested in the spiritual realities at the center of his life.

He went to the Cross because his very goodness was repellent to so many of his fellows. Those who love evil always hate goodness. This is one of the facts of life and religion. It explains why the prophets and early religious leaders were stoned and put to death. It helps to explain why Jesus, too, went to Calvary. His own goodness antagonized people who were unwilling to accept his spirit for their lives.

They crucified Jesus because he was too good! Evil hates goodness. We often dislike people who refuse to be used by us, if we are arbitrary enough to insist that they do our will. The man who has been your friend may become your enemy, if you refuse to comply with the rigid demand that he makes upon you. Unless he has a love for goodness, and a sense of fair play, he will most likely turn against you. Arbitrary individuals who are deeply prejudiced want others to conform to their desires. That is what the religious leaders wanted Jesus to do, but he refused to heed them.

People who were once friendly toward us sometimes come to hate us because we are not willing to be dictated to by them. When we lay this fact down beside that other truth of which we were thinking, namely, that evil hates goodness, we get a glimpse of the inevitability of the Cross. We see something about it that is so graphic it sweeps across our minds with a flash. The fellow-citizens of Amos hated the prophet because he loved the poor people. Others hated Micah because he told them thousands of rams, offered in sacrifice, would not serve as a substitute for justice. The Pharisees did not like Jesus. How could they unless they changed!

"But woe unto you, scribes and Pharisees, hypocrites! for ye shut up the kingdom of heaven against men: for

18

ye neither go in yourselves, neither suffer ye them that are entering to go in.

"Woe unto you, scribes and Pharisees, hypocrites! for ye devour widows' houses, and for a pretence make long prayers: therefore ye shall receive the greater damnation.

"Woe unto you, scribes and Pharisees, hypocrites! for ye compass sea and land to make one proselyte; and when he is made, ye make him twofold more the child of hell than yourselves. . . . .

"Woe unto you, scribes and Pharisees, hypocrites! for ye pay tithe of mint, and anise, and cummin, and have omitted the weightier matters of the law, judgment, mercy, and faith: these ought ye to have done, and not to leave the other undone. . . . .

"Woe unto you, scribes and Pharisees, hypocrites! because ye build the tombs of the prophets, and garnish the sepulchres of the righteous, and say, if we had been in the days of our fathers, we would not have been partakers with them in the blood of the prophets. Wherefore ye be witnesses unto yourselves, that ye are the children of them which killed the prophets."

How could people hear these words and not become bitterly angry—unless they repented of their sins!

If we who are ministers were to preach with such

uncompromising vehemence, our churches would have more empty pews! Most people simply cannot face facts that have to do with their unethical relationships. To do so is too painful. The people could not stand this Man who stood on the street corner and told them of their sins, who walked out before them and said: "Ye serpents, ye generation of vipers! how can ye escape the damnation of hell? Wherefore, behold, I send unto you prophets, and wise men, and scribes: and some of them ye shall kill and crucify; and some of them shall ye scourge in your synagogues, and persecute them from city to city."

The self-righteous could not stand that. We could not stand it today. People still turn against the man who challenges them with uncompromising truth like that. Jesus went to the Cross because there were those conditions—personal and social—which forced him to the Cross.

If Jesus were to come again, we would kill him. We might not nail him to a cross. We might shoot him or hang him. Crucifixions no longer take place as they did in Jesus' day. But we would kill Jesus! There is something so terrible about personal resentment and mass psychology that when we begin to realize that a man has spoken too plainly to us, something rises up within us, like some surging power, and we demand vengeance. We join the hosts who insist upon punishment for one who has offended us.

Why the Cross? The Cross had to be, simply because there was anger and hatred and ugliness which rose up against Jesus. All these were in the minds and hearts of the people to whom Christ spoke. The Cross is simply inescapable when you have a prophet, like Jesus, who will not run away because he is brave enough to stay. The Cross is unavoidable when you have a Righteous Man who insists that goodness triumph, and people who violently oppose the kind of goodness for which he pleads.

III

But much more is involved! Jesus talked of God in terms that the religious leaders of his own day could neither understand nor appreciate. He was the mouthpiece of this Deity. He was the one who delivered the message of God. Furthermore, he actually lived everything he taught. The people did not like that. They did not want a Godlike Leader, one who loved all alike, regardless of race, color, or social caste.

If Jesus could have overlooked the conditions of his day, no one would have been offended. *He could have been a popular pastor!* But, as soon as he began to speak of social injustices, as soon as he probed into the deeper motives of the human heart, they began to plan how to be rid of Jesus. The truth cut them to the quick. They did not want to hear about *sin*.

So they carried Jesus out to the Cross. They made a terrific mistake. They should have asked how to be free from sin, and how to learn the meaning of divine forgiveness, and then how to experience it. They needed the truth—and divine grace—to set them free!

Christ was so earnest in his thinking, so uncompromising in his dealing that necessarily only those who were willing to accept him would be his friends. The rest became his enemies.

IV

There is something so challenging in this experience of Jesus that we may well despair of ever fully understanding it. We need, however, to bring as much as possible of its truth to our life today. We need to see that the same forces still run directly athwart the divine purposes of Christ. We honor him ritualistically, but we go right on opposing him ethically and morally.

That is a disturbing story which Francis Turner Palgrave, the compiler of *The Golden Treasury,* tells in his diary, describing the behavior of the mob that invaded the Palace of the Tuileries during the French Revolution. The mob had gone through several rooms. They were intent upon looting and destroying what they saw. It was a violent, shrieking crowd of enraged people. They burst open a closed door, to find themselves suddenly in the palace chapel. There above the altar was an appropriate painting. It was of Christ being crucified. A hush fell upon this furious crowd of enraged men. Somebody cried out, "Hats off!" Every head was bowed. Then before one realized what was occurring, the crowd knelt. Reverence and awe laid hold upon them.

Then in the silence of that holy reverence, somebody went forward and took down the picture from the altar. It was placed in a neighboring church. But when the picture was removed, the tide of destruction rolled on.

It is almost too vivid a scene upon which to meditate. We are so very much like that! Last Sunday we looked at the Cross. Somewhere next Sunday we shall see the Cross and become very reverent in its presence. We will face it again and again, and then forget the Man who hung on it. Or we will go out and crucify him again.

The same evil is in control of the hearts of men as

was dominant in the first Christian century. Jesus goes to Calvary again because there are conditions that sweep him to the Cross and nail him there. *We* nail him there.

I am thinking about a man now who for a number of years has kept saying that he honors the Christ. In many ways he has said that he feels the Master is worthy of his soul. In a letter he indicates the same fact again. I know he feels the Christ should have his heart and life, but at the close of his brief message he says he cannot now make Christ his king. He refuses to give the Master his heart. When I last talked with him, as I looked in his face, I made an earnest appeal. But he turned back from accepting the Christ. Resolutely, through the years, he has walked across the soul of Jesus Christ; and yet he takes off his hat before the altar, and in the sacred sanctuary he can be as reverent as you and I.

Devoted church people forced Jesus to Golgotha and compelled the soldiers to nail him to the Cross. They were people who knew enough about religion to be reverent. They had read the Hebrew psalms and were familiar with the religion of their day. "Our God is an awful God," said the Hebrews. That was part of their

24

religion—a sense of holy awe. They felt it then, but they still carried Jesus out and crucified him.

He is still suffering. Look at the hosts who refuse to respond to his appeal. Look into your own heart —and mine—and see how we have crushed this Lover of our souls.

Sometime ago I sat in a church pew with a man to whom I was talking about this same Christ of the Cross. The man was reverent and polite. He was willing to go to church. That in itself is better than hosts of people are doing today. He had a sense of what was right. He could be prayerful in church. But he would not do anything about the Cross, and when he walked out he tramped deliberately across the Christ's soul. I saw him again. There were written on his face deep lines that spoke volumes concerning the failures of his life.

v

Jesus went to the Cross long before he trudged up the hill of Golgotha. Let us keep that in mind.

See him as he stands outside the city walls. At least spiritually, he looks upon the whole city as he cries, "O Jerusalem, Jerusalem . . . . how often would I have gathered thy children together, as a hen doth gather her brood under her wings, and ye would not!" It is the torture of rejected Love—the suffering of one who could save, and who longed to redeem, but whose proffer of aid was ruthlessly rejected.

"I sometimes think about the cross,
    And shut my eyes and try to see
The cruel nails and crown of thorns,
    And Jesus crucified for me.

"But even could I see him die,
    I could but see a little part
Of that great love which like a fire
    Is always burning in his heart."

Nevertheless, we do see quite vividly something of the greatness in his soul! As he hung on the cross, many others went by and wagged their heads. They laughed at Jesus and scornfully shook their heads, saying, "Why don't you come down from the cross? Once you could do many miracles. You saved others; save yourself!" It all seemed ludicrous to them. It was a laughable matter.

You can tell what people are by what amuses them. How we treat sacred things, seriously or humorously, discloses something of our deepest character. They laughed at Jesus. That hurt him more than all their cruel, bitter words. The reason has to do with his love

26

for them. They broke his heart. That spiritual tragedy was enacted many times before he went to Calvary!

Jesus refused to follow any other way except the
course of Divine Love. Certain disciples once wished
that he would call down fire from heaven and burn up
a village that failed to welcome him; but Jesus did not
adopt that technique. He would not compel people
to do right. Nor would he call twelve legions of
angels to deliver him from his enemies.

There was a Cross in the soul of Jesus before he went
to Golgotha. It was because he loved these people.
So, too, because he loves you and me, *when we play the
fool, it kills him!* His soul is crushed when we will
have nothing to do with all that he offers in order to
redeem us.

Suppose you were a physician—suppose a man whose
life you were trying to save, who was not under the influence of an anesthetic and was altogether in his rational mind, hated you for trying to help him. Suppose you were operating upon this man, working desperately, and while he was completely rational he
said vehement, violent, mean things to you all the
time, and yet you kept trying to save his life. The
man laughs at you, spits in your face, and does every-

27

thing in his power to distract your attention, and to turn you from what you are doing. He thinks you are quite silly. He sneers at you for wanting to save him. That is a faint picture of what these people were doing who laughed at Jesus.

Rénan pens a picture of Jesus on Calvary, rejected by the very people he came to save. He raises the question as to whether Christ may have repented at the very hour that he was dying for such ungrateful people—so vile a race! The pitiless eastern sun is beating down upon him. The crowd, half mocking and half compassionate, is surging at his feet. The Roman soldiers are gambling to see who will have his last possessions. It may be that the voice of the tempter did then whisper in his ear, "To what purpose is all this?" But Jesus went on anyway, and died because he loved man that much. When the night came, it was not dark enough to hide the most unselfish deed the world has ever witnessed. Here was the lifeless body of a Man who had lived more devotedly for humanity than any individual who has ever walked the roadways of this world!

Why the Cross? The evils of the human heart compelled Christ to go to Calvary. Yet even with all the sins that made it necessary, it gave Jesus the marvelous chance of saying something everlastingly real about the Heart of the universe. Some of us are sure that because Christ suffered, as he lived, on our level of life, we can truly love God; and we thus discover the power to rise toward him. *Choosing the Cross—with all it means—was more like God than anything else Christ could have done!*

JUDAS, WHO BETRAYED HIM

Then entered Satan into Judas surnamed Iscariot, being of the number of the twelve. And he went his way, and communed with the chief priests and captains, how he might betray him unto them.

—LUKE 22:3, 4

No ONE INDIVIDUAL WAS RESPONSIBLE FOR THE DEATH of Jesus. His crucifixion was not so simple a matter as that! There were many who had a part in his torture. On one occasion there seemed to be a multitude that could scarcely be numbered.

Whoever else we may hold answerable, however, we cannot excuse Judas. Everybody associates him with the death of Jesus. No matter what our honest beliefs may be about who was chiefly responsible, it is impossible to dismiss the betrayal of Judas from our minds when we recall the bloody experience of the Cross. Indeed, when we were quite young, many of us felt that if we could have taken Judas out of the story, we might not have had the Cross. Somehow we were convinced that he was of all men most guilty.

Among other reasons for our feeling this way, there is one that is easily overlooked. It is the fact that Judas is referred to as a traitor on several occasions in the New Testament. When the name of Judas is used by three biblical writers, they add a clause with which every reader of the New Testament is familiar. It is this: "who also betrayed him." Long before the crucifixion, the reader is told that Judas is going to have this despicable part in the tragedy of the Cross. Sometimes one feels an injustice has been done the man. The reader is prejudiced against him, even in the earlier pages of the record.

I

That is not fair. We ought happily to recognize every fine quality the man portrayed. Certainly Judas must have had many admirable traits of character. There was undoubtedly much that was most attractive about him. Otherwise Jesus would never have chosen him for a disciple. Furthermore, Judas was a man of ability. It is not reasonable to think that Jesus would have entrusted him with the funds of the company unless he had had some sound intelligence concerning finances. It is a compliment to Judas that Jesus permitted him to become the treasurer of this first Christian group. Undoubtedly, if we had seen Judas when he first became a disciple of Jesus, we would have liked him. We would have been sure that Jesus had made another wise selection.

Indeed, it is altogether reasonable to assume that Judas had a spirit of idealism. Otherwise, he would not have become an intimate friend of Jesus. There must have been devotion and love for the Master in the heart of Judas. It is not good judgment to assert that he could have followed Jesus and lived with him through all the months of his ministry without being affected by the magnetic qualities of the Master of men.

Of course, there are some people who think that Judas must have had some dishonorable purpose in his heart from the outset. The facts do not sustain this theory. Judas chose Jesus because he was interested in what Jesus proposed to do. Furthermore, he undoubtedly enjoyed being in the company of this remarkable Man. In his choice of Jesus, Judas was displaying real interest and enthusiasm for a cause that had captivated his thinking, even though he did not fully understand it.

There can scarcely be any doubt of the fact that Judas was a true disciple, at least for a while. Remember that Judas made the same sacrifice that Peter and James and John made. He left all to follow Jesus. He shared the toils of the Master for the many months

32

he was with him. He went through the same trials.
Is it reasonable to suppose that he was nursing black
trickery in his heart all this time? Even to ask the
question is to have the answer. It is entirely contrary
to reason to think that this would have been true.
Judas was capable of high idealism. To be sure, there
was a bad streak in him. But in whom is there not
a bad streak, or at least something that can easily de-
velop into one?

We cannot even pretend to know just when Judas
succumbed to the temptation which finally defeated
him. Just how his mind became so warped that he
could entertain the thought of trickery is something we
shall likely never know. He made his mistake when
he allowed himself to dwell upon the dark thoughts
that came to his mind until, after a while, they dominated his thinking.

Just how soon love of money mastered Judas, we do
not know. But the time came when he did not want
to see money wasted as he believed the woman was
wasting it who expressed her ardent affection with expensive perfume. The idea of one's being so devoted
to another that one could only portray it by means of
free-hearted generosity did not appeal to Judas.

But let no one hastily condemn his interest in money.

33

Who has not been deeply interested either in money or what money can do for one? It is how one gains it, what one does with it, and why one spends it as one does, or why one gives it away, and to whom, that counts most. Who has not wished for the security and independence which finances seem to be able to guarantee? In one of our modern novels there is a character who wanted riches in order that he might be able to tell certain of his enemies that they could go to the devil. Many a man has felt that temptation too!

Sometimes we feel very painfully the way many people quibble about money, when it could be used for a worthy purpose, and when those who are able to direct its use refuse to be generous. Some time ago a friend of mine was telling about a minister whom I had known and admired, who received a call to a certain educational institution. During the time he was pondering over what he should do, he had a conference with his church officials about a proposed expenditure for the church that was quite inexpensive. It was one to which they should have given their attention with interest and appreciation. As he watched these men quibble over a few dollars, his thinking concerning his new opportunity crystallized. He walked out of the meeting, feeling impelled to take the new position. He could not stand the continued emphasis on money by people who were able to be generous, but who refused to portray real Christianity in their decisions concerning the church.

This thing of money has so many angles and it makes so many subtle appeals that few of us can look scornfully at Judas with the assurance that we are altogether superior to him in his false evaluation of things material. As has been pointed out, Judas was not the first, nor the last, treasurer of a religious group who vehemently denounced the prodigality of love. When he revolted against the idea of waste in this demonstration of generous love at Bethany, it was not because the needs of the poor pressed heavily upon his mind and heart. Things had not gone to please him. And whatever avarice there was in his soul had nourished other evil desires and attitudes.

We have recently been told of a millionaire at whose funeral there was sung the song, "There's a Gold Mine in the Sky." It is, indeed, to be earnestly hoped that the song was a slander on the man's character. But anyone who permits covetousness to become the master of his life, will scarcely be able to think of any future being worth while without some kind of gold mine.

Judas had simply reached the place he could not

see the most lovely things in life. Whether he had actually been stealing money from the treasury is not a primary consideration. His soul withered long before his body died. Jesus had seen the changes gradually coming over the man. But the Master kept treating Judas with gracious courtesy and tender love. It was the only way Jesus knew how to deal with anyone. It was the method he adopted for all those with whom he lived.

Of course, Jesus might have told Judas he would have no more to do with him, thus excluding him from the intimate fellowship both of the disciples and of himself. Had he chosen to do so, he might have forced Judas to announce his purpose, to disclose his plan. But none of these indicates the technique of Jesus. With a heart filled with love for the man, he had to watch him shrivel up spiritually and die religiously, even while he did everything within the compass of Heaven's power—which is divine love—to save him.

II

Whatever the rapidity with which Judas reached his decision, the time came when he was ready to betray Jesus. He went to the religious authorities. He bargained with them. The price upon which they agreed was thirty pieces of silver. The priests would have undoubtedly paid a much higher sum for Jesus. That is why some people think jealousy was one of the impelling motives that caused Jud~ his Master.

Dr. Alfred Adler has told of a little girl of six who became very delicate and as a result of her ill health was the petted member of her home. Then a baby sister was born. It was hard on the older child because she found herself no longer the center of her parents' interest. Her jealousy became so intense that she lost control of herself. One day the body of a little child was found in a brook near the village where this six-year-old girl lived. Later another child was found in the same brook. As a result of careful watch, to the startling surprise of everyone concerned, this little girl of six was caught in the act of throwing a third baby girl into the water. A shocking story, to be sure, but it is a powerful suggestion as to what extreme jealousy and envy can carry one.

It is possible that Judas was a Judean, and therefore was afflicted with a sense of superiority. It may be that he asked himself whether he had been made a fool by all the humiliating circumstances of his discipleship. Doubtless, there were many motives that played in on

37

the man's mind and heart. Certainly, money was not the only one, if, indeed, it was the primary one.

Judas may have felt Jesus could have done more for him. Sometimes an assassin will kill a statesman who represents for him a father who has been responsible for his regrettable position in life. A prominent psychiatrist has pointed out that nearly all assassins are poor. He shows how the prominent person who is slain is quite often, psychically, the assassin's father. Referring to this strange situation, John Gunther points out that Brutus, for instance, may have killed Caesar because as his spiritual son he wanted to be closest to Caesar's heart and saw that he was being displaced by Mark Antony. There are those who believe that Brutus murdered Caesar, not because he hated him, but because he was jealous of him.

Some say that Judas was always a devil in spite of his attractive personality. But this assertion is actually a slander on Jesus. It is thoroughly unreasonable—it is an indictment of Jesus' character—to suggest that he would have chosen an emissary of the nether world for his disciple.

Judas could not possibly have betrayed Jesus lightly. His motive was certainly a far deeper matter than simply trying to earn a little bit of extra money. **Fur-**

ermore, even after Judas had succumbed to the temptation, there was still much good left in him. The appalling remorse which gripped his mind and heart is a clear indication of the fact that there was still something noble about the man.

There are some who, far from harshly condemning Judas, assert that he was a saint who was lacking in understanding. He was trying to compel Jesus to become an earthly Messiah. The facts, however, do not confirm this theory. Even though there is the possibility that he was attempting to force the hand of Jesus, and show that Christ was a man of divine power, the true Messiah, it is still not possible to call Judas a saint!

Some say that he was chosen in order that he might be the traitor. It is certainly not like the Christ of Gethsemane and of Calvary to choose a man for the purpose of betraying any individual. Even to think of Jesus' planning from the beginning of his ministry that Judas should be the one to betray him is almost blasphemous. Far from this, Jesus treated the man with gracious tenderness and divine compassion. That was the only way he could be Christly.

Nevertheless, Judas followed his traitorous course, and turned against the Master of his heart and life. He bartered with Jesus' enemies. He went out with the group to take Jesus. There is no way to excuse him. He was responsible for what he was doing.

A number of years ago, a murderer in England went to his death to expiate for his crime; at the same time another man was arrested who was responsible for three deaths. On trial this man told the court how, as a druggist, on the night when he mistakenly made up his poisonous prescriptions which had caused the three deaths, he had been nursing his wife for three days and nights. She was dangerously ill. He was nervously distracted. For two days he had had no sleep. When he made up his prescriptions he thought a bottle of poison was distilled water. As a result of his "crime" he was sentenced for manslaughter, but only for a brief imprisonment. Deep sympathy was extended by many who heard of his suffering. The consequence of these two acts was the same, namely, death. But the first was heinous and black in the deepest way of which we can think, because it was purposed. It was planned. The second man had no intention of killing another.

Judas knew he was betraying Jesus. We cannot excuse him!

It was a silly sight—this band of armed men who

came to capture an unarmed man who had always refused to protect himself, who had always refused to fight. He himself said that he could have called a legion of angels, but this he refused to do. Look at that motley band of armed men as they come with staves and swords and lanterns to take the Christ, who only a few moments ago was kneeling in prayer!

So Judas betrays him with a kiss. A rattlesnake warns his victim. Judas did not. He kissed the Man he came to betray. We remember the maiden who put poison on her lips in order to murder the man who responded to her ardent appeals of love.

The kiss Judas gave Jesus was a sign of discipleship. Students were accustomed to kiss their rabbi. For Judas to use this symbol of affection in the way that he did cut the heart of Jesus far more deeply than even Jesus ever suggested. It surely pained him more than did the blows of the soldiers. What heart-rending words they were Christ had used earlier: "Behold, the hand of him that betrayeth me is with me on the table." Satan had entered the soul of Judas.

After it was all over, Judas wanted to undo what he had done. He flung the silver that he had taken at the feet of those with whom he had bargained. He was tormented with the memory of having betrayed the best Friend he ever had. He could have repented, but he did not. With marked restraint the statement is made that he went unto his own place.

III

Why the Cross? *There was Judas, who betrayed Jesus!* He was responsible. He is certainly one of those upon whom we have to place the responsibility. There is no way to excuse him.

Why the Cross? Because there are still people like Judas, people who deceive their own friends, people who practice chicanery with the sons and daughters of God. There are those today who stab others in the back with false insinuations and bitter accusations. Professing friends whom we cannot trust can still wound us deeply.

The method of Judas is not out of date. He vividly shows us how we too inflict pain upon others who are also God's children. We still know how to get rid of our enemies, or at least how to bring intense suffering upon their souls. Judas did dramatically what many others have done in more subtle ways, with friends of Jesus.

There are still those who refuse to respond to the loving appeal of a divine Christ, or who turn against this one to whom once they gave themselves with the idealistic devotion of young dreamers who have seen the highest and want to make it their very own.

There are still hosts of us who by some kiss of professed allegiance and devotion indicate our loyalty to the finest things in life, but who permit lust for financial gain, or political ambition for worldly prestige, or inordinate desire for social advancement, to be the real motive of our souls. To pose as a friend of Jesus, or of his cause, and then let the mixed motives of desire for place or power to control us and actually direct our lives, is to betray Jesus again with a kiss.

> "Was it for sins that I have done,
> He suffered on the tree?
> Amazing pity! grace unknown!
> And love beyond degree!"

SIMON PETER, WHO LOST HIS NERVE

And Peter remembered the word of Jesus, which said unto him, Before the cock crow, thou shalt deny me thrice. And he went out, and wept bitterly.

—MATTHEW 26:75

IF IT WERE NECESSARY FOR US TO ACCEPT PART OF THE responsibility for the crucifixion of Jesus, probably most of us would prefer being classified with Simon Peter. Certainly we like to feel that we are much closer spiritually to him than we are to Judas. We have a marked antipathy to Judas. We are quite friendly toward Simon Peter, even though he did deny Jesus. We always remember that he later repented. Furthermore, when we recall what a strong character this disciple became, we realize we are complimenting ourselves in a subtle way by claiming kinship with him.

I

There was undoubtedly always love and devotion in the heart of Simon Peter for his Master. Even when the disciples fled following the betrayal by Judas, Peter and John seem to have regained their own courage, at least to some extent. Peter followed him afar off.

44

Many harsh criticisms of Peter have been based on this incident. The biblical account has served as the basis for many sermons. Simon has been heartily condemned for following the Master afar off. Most of these statements of condemnation are entirely too severe and altogether out of order. Peter was at least following his Master! At that very moment all the others had apparently forsaken him. What he did was certainly far better than complete desertion.

Finally Peter came to the Oriental house where Jesus was waiting. The house was built around the paved courtyard. A friendly act of a fellow disciple secured entree for Simon. John was able to get him in. He passed the outer gate where there was a room, or some kind of lodge, for the porter. He went through the wicket gate that was opened and shut by a porter.

Then he strolled toward the group where they were discussing this Strange Man called Jesus. The Master was being condemned by everyone. Nobody was lifting a voice of protest, or speaking a word of commendation for Jesus. The crowd was set against him. Peter might have recalled an ancient Hebrew psalm with which he was doubtless familiar. He could have well repeated those words to himself: "Blessed is the man that walketh not in the counsel of the ungodly, nor standeth in the way of sinners, nor sitteth in the seat of the scornful." But Peter forgot those words, or refused to meditate upon them.

He was cold, for the night air had chilled his body; and there was a fire in the center of the courtyard. He went over to warm himself. The courtyard was ringing with jests about Jesus. He was the butt of many crude jokes. The crowd was laughing at this ridiculous man whom some had foolishly claimed was the Messiah. Simon kept silent. It is possible that he tried to appear as though he were one of the scorners. At least, he was not willing to make a protest, and that meant that already he was in imminent danger. For not to confess our devotion for one to whom we have sworn our loyalty is the next thing to denying him. Peter, however, had not forgotten his Lord. How could he ever forget Christ?

There may be a few people who deliberately tear themselves away from religion, but most of those who deny religion by word of mouth deep down in their hearts are convinced that it is one of life's realities. Most people do secretly cultivate some sense of religion. The trouble with too many of us, however, is that we try to serve two masters. This was Simon Peter's difficulty. Down deep in his soul he was still secretly worshiping Jesus, but he wanted to be popular with the crowd. He could smile at their witticisms. He could laugh as they laughed. He did not want to be treated as a peculiar individual who stood out against the crowd.

II

Then came this sudden and severe attack on his sense of loyalty from an altogether unexpected source. Probably already there had been suspicious glances toward Simon. Some had doubtless been glaring at him, wondering who he was, and why he was there. With a woman's cleverness, a portress had evidently discerned the secret that Peter was trying so desperately to keep hidden in his own heart. As she passed by, on the way to her room, this woman glanced at Peter with a twinkle in her eyes and said to the soldiers who were standing there, "This is one of the Nazarene's followers." There was scorn in her voice. She did not even try to hide her malicious spirit. It was quite amusing to her that anyone should be a follower of this man who was so weak he could not protect himself. He had been betrayed and now was ready to be condemned. Peter was taken by surprise. Fear laid hold on his heart.

He had already gone too far in his cowardly course.

For he had listened to the crowd make fun of Jesus. They may have even blasphemed him. He had sat there in the company, or stood with them, and heard their ribald remarks without making a single protest. Now he was too intricately involved to extricate himself. He said, quite simply: "I do not know what you mean." Fear had won in the battle for Peter's soul. He did not have the courage to express his real feelings, to be true to his truest self. He had lost his nerve.

Who does not sympathize with him? How many times we have been afraid that people would laugh at us! Or we have been troubled with the thought of violent disagreement. Some of us still fear what certain people will say about us. We can understand the mind of Simon Peter.

But Peter is not done with this matter. He is now more than uncomfortable; he is quite nervous. He turns away from every suspicious glance. Cowardice has already laid hold upon him. The ghosts of fear are stalking through the corridors of his soul. He has denied his Master, and every moment that passes is like the tide of the sea carrying him further and further out, so that he cannot save himself.

There is another maiden standing near. She comes

near him. She may have been out at the gate through which he had to pass in order to reach the inner court. She also accuses him, saying, "That is one of the followers of this Nazarene." Now the man is more than irritated. He cannot stand what is going on. A sense of guilt sweeps through his conscience. It is simply overpowering. He has already lied once. He turns around and lies again, this time with an oath. Then he turns abruptly and warms himself again by the fire.

His body may be finding comfort, but there is another fire that does not comfort him. It is raging within his soul. It is burning his very heart out. No one who knows this man Simon Peter can imagine that he was able to stay still, even physically, for a little while. Why don't these people attend to their own affairs? But they will not leave him alone.

There was another who recognized him. The panic-stricken man simply lost all control of himself. He was now like a maddened animal who was being attacked. He doubtless felt that they were dealing with him unfairly. There is scarcely any doubt, either, but that he could justify what he had done. It was the only thing to do under the circumstances, he may have told himself. "A man could not play the fool, and run the risk of being arrested himself. He could do Jesus so much more good as a free man." But a tempest is raging in his heart. There are loud accusations. How he wishes they would hush! Blind with rage, he swears with an oath that he does not know this man. Then the cock crows. It is like the sounding of the knell that summons a man to his death.

Why had Peter lost his nerve? He did not have to show the white feather. Let us never forget this. He could have assumed another attitude from the very moment he entered the courtyard. He might have made a decision similar to that made by one of our well-known religious leaders a number of years ago. The incident which concerned him occurred at a club in one of our great cities. The occasion was a special gathering that had brought together a number of prominent citizens. A nationally known politician presided. An internationally known military officer from England was a special guest. The well-known politician was forceful and strong in presenting the worthy cause that had already won the interest of the group. Those who were present at the dinner were most responsive and cordial.

There was one great embarrassment in the meeting, however, which sorely disturbed at least one man present, the minister. The chairman kept using violent and profane language which was in direct contrast to the spirit of religion, that emphasizes genuine reverence.

Then the clergyman was most graciously introduced by the politician. In his introduction he remarked that he had sat up until midnight reading a volume of the man's sermons. His wife had presented him with the copy. In responding, the noted clergyman told how interested he was in the project which was being discussed that evening. He pointed out how worthy he considered it. But he went on to add that if he had had the least idea that the chairman was going to sit up and read a volume of his sermons, he would have certainly included one on profanity.

Of course the group laughed, in both an open and a half-concealed manner. The chairman looked at his feet and at last said: "Doctor, I guess I had it coming to me!"

This clergyman, whom some of us admire greatly, asserted that it was one of those occasions where to let the matter pass in silence would have been either stupidity or cowardice.

The statement suggests exactly what happened with Simon Peter. He did take the stupid and cowardly course. He could have avoided all the difficulty which he later faced if he had only testified as to his allegiance and loyalty to Jesus. But he let his chance go by, and as a result had to pay the price of painful remorse.

III

All this would have been enough. He now is wounded in his soul beyond words. But there is something far more painful for him. *He sees Jesus! And Jesus says nothing!* The Master does not accuse him or condemn him. The Master does not utter a single harshly spoken word. In his countenance are only disappointment, pity, sorrow, and divine love. There is deep pathos in his soul and—forgiveness! Even Peter can see that on the face of Jesus.

In his book, *Jesus, The Son of Man,* Kahlil Gibran says that when the Master warned Peter that he would betray him, he "put his hand upon Peter's shoulder, and smiled upon him, and said, 'Who knows but that you may deny me before this night is over and leave me before I leave you?'" Here was warning, but given, so Gibran thinks, with the smile of a devoted friend.

It crushed Simon Peter now to see what Jesus still thought of him. It hurt him when he realized how tenderly the Master was going to deal with him, in spite of all the bitterness with which he had denied his Friend. *That look of Christ broke his heart.*

52

It was the look which also rescued him. Peter realized that Jesus still loved him. He understood that Jesus would forgive him. The look of Christ was more than enough to tell him how terribly he had failed. But that look also gave him his one great hope—that Christ would extend his divine pardon if he repented. There was more than keen disappointment in the eyes of Jesus. *There was the love of the Saviour.*

That is why Peter did not stop with remorse; he went on to repentance. He turned his back upon the past. He sought the redeeming forgiveness of his Lord. It was too late to change the past. The moving finger had already written and then moved on. All the regret and all the remorse of Peter could not change it. But Peter knew that he could write again, yes, write a far better record under the direction of Jesus. He went out to inscribe a message on the hearts and minds of men that they could never forget. If Jesus could forgive him, Simon Peter, then Jesus could redeem any man! That he could say to every despairing soul.

When some of us see how the heart of Simon Peter was cut to the quick, we remember many deeds in our own lives which we keenly regret. Who cannot recall many things that he wishes he could change? How we have suffered because we failed to play the man! Sometimes we feel salty tears coming to our eyes because we disappointed our parents. Now that we have children of our own, we understand how we grieved them. We are deeply pained.

Boswell tells us how when Samuel Johnson was only a boy, he once refused to go to the Uttoxeter Market at the direction of his father. His father kept a bookstall in this marketplace, and he earnestly desired his boy's help. As a proud laddie, who did not feel obedience was to be expected at the time, Samuel Johnson refused to go. It was only a momentary act of disobedience. It occurred in his early boyhood. But Dr. Johnson never forgot it. The memory of it made deep lines in his mind. When he was an old man, in order to help his own feelings, as a symbol of his repentance, Samuel Johnson went back to the marketplace and stood there bareheaded in the rain in the very spot where his father's bookstall had been. Simon Peter could have understood Johnson's feelings. Johnson knew something at least of the pathetic state of Peter's heart.

IV

Why the Cross? Well, there was Simon Peter whose denial brought unutterable anguish to the soul of Jesus, hours before the wooden beams were erected outside

54

the city walls. No one likes to have a friend deny that he knows him. The deeper our friendship goes, the more severe is our suffering when one turns against us. Peter had sworn the allegiance of his soul to Jesus. He had declared that though all others should deny Jesus, he most positively would not. But he did!

Why the Cross? Because there are still hosts of us who formally profess Christianity, and then in one way or another, by attitudes and deeds, deny that we are followers of Jesus. We may have once sworn allegiance, but then we turn against him. We warm ourselves by some fire where a group is gathered, sneering at sacred things or laughing at religion. We offer no protest. By one gesture or another we deny that we belong to Christ. We sit with some group in the smoker on the pullman. From what we say and do, no one would ever guess that we had knelt at the holy communion altar and worshiped the Christ who died upon a Cross. We deny that we know him.

We well know that we cannot afford to compromise our souls. We have promised not to do so. But since everybody else is indulging, we do too. We sit with the cynics. We laugh with the scorners. We joke with the sneerers. We never raise our voice in protest when thrusts are being made at the highest and holiest things

55

in life; and after a while, when we have become so deeply involved there is no way out, and someone raises the question about our religious loyalties, we become irritable and vehemently deny that we are puritanical. We are men and women of the world. We are quite sophisticated. We can take care of ourselves. We are not narrow. We are quite liberal—liberal enough to deny that we are Christ's followers!

Why the Cross? Because there are people like you and me who still deny the Christ!

TWO SHREWD POLITICIANS: ANNAS AND CAIAPHAS

Then the band . . . . took Jesus, and bound him, and led
him away to Annas first . . . . Annas . . . . sent him bound
unto Caiaphas.

—JOHN 18:12, 13, 24

ANNAS AND JESUS! WHAT A STRANGE MEETING! HERE
were two men, representing religion, who were as far
apart as the two poles. Jesus had said that true religion
makes one self-sacrificing. Annas had used even the
church for selfish purposes.

Annas was no stranger to Jesus. When Jesus was
only a boy, helping his father in the carpenter's shop
in Nazareth, Annas was high priest. The best people
had not been drawn to him. By his very nature he
repelled those who had a high sense of ethics. He had
been a man of power who knew how to use it ruthlessly. Annas was haughty and proud. Those who
have studied his life assert he was also cruel. He did
not refrain from making others suffer. After a number of years he was removed from office.

The influence of Annas, however, remained. He was
a shrewd church politician who knew how to accom-

plish most of his purposes. By clever manipulating he had remained the real power of Israel. He had been able to secure the office of high priesthood for four sons. Caiaphas, who was high priest at the time of Jesus' crucifixion, was the son-in-law of Annas. Wire-pulling had become an art with Annas. As James Black has said, by means of it he had made the highest office in the Jewish religion practically a family possession.

The Jewish law and system of religion had played into the hands of this unscrupulous politician. Once a year each Israelite had to journey to the Holy Temple, bringing what was known as "the price of atonement." Since the law required that this half-shekel be offered in the coin known as the shekel of the sanctuary, it was necessary for the people to exchange the money they normally used for this special currency. The money-changers had tables at convenient places so that the offering of redemption would be available in the proper coin. A fee was charged for every transaction. Thus the profit from the service rendered amounted to thousands of dollars in our money. Religion had become quite expensive!

There was also a charge made for examining the objects which were used at the Passover feast, such as the lambs brought by the peasants. These necessary items were also provided for those who did not bring them. The price placed on them was as high as the public would pay. The profit on these concessions added to the wealth and power of Annas and his family. The ex-high priest, having established the system, saw that the funds were properly "directed." Annas was a shrewd business man.

Like some other clever possessors of power who are not particularly eager to hold high offices themselves, but who insist on controlling those who are in places of supposed authority, Annas knew how to direct human puppets. He was adept at making others do what he said. He was old in years, but, as has been pointed out, he was still older in cunning. His was a serpentine wisdom. Some have thought he had no sense of honor whatever, nor any regard at all for the rights of others. His conscience may have spoken to him, *but Annas did not confer with it.* His obstinacy was too pronounced to permit any consideration of the feelings of others to determine what he did.

Everybody recognized his power. The band who had gone out to take Jesus hurried their captive to Annas first of all. This was a clear recognition of his political power. It was a tribute to the ecclesiastical prestige of this underhanded manipulator of church machinery. Men knew that he was the real ruler of Israel.

I

Two entirely different principles of life are personified in the meeting of Jesus and Annas. How vividly they are portrayed! Here was an old man who thought of everything and everybody in terms of how he could use them. His aims and purposes had to do with material things. Though he practiced his cunning under the guise of religion, he did not believe in the reality of the unseen. His life was not guided by high religious ideals. Seventy-year-old Annas was convinced that only place and power and prestige counted. Possessions were worth more than a sense of honor.

Now he was looking upon a man whose whole life was guided by the everlasting principles of right. Here was Jesus facing him, who had said that a man should be willing to give up every material possession, if need be, in order to keep his conscience clear. Annas did not know how to do anything "out in the open." Jesus was never ashamed of anything he did. He was willing for everything in the records of his life to be read by everybody. Jesus was clear in his thinking, honest in his purposes and plans, and always went straight as an arrow toward his goal of goodness. He was uncompromisingly devoted to truth and love. Annas had lived in secret conference rooms and had used people who were willing to do what he told them in order to gain some little recognition or economic security.

Some time ago I was in another state, where I had gone for a series of special religious services. A friend of mine, a college president, was discussing a character in that city, now old and very lonely. He had once been the most powerful church politician of his denomination in the particular area in which he lived. He had been able to get things done. He knew how to promote those in whom he was interested. For years what he said counted with many people. Now he was old and lonely. Those who might have been his comrades had no reason to be friendly. He had not displayed the warmth of friendship in his earlier years. Those who might have cared for him remembered how he had once manipulated church machinery.

It is a faint picture of Annas, except that in his old age he was still the man of power he had been. He was still in the place of influence. Even the masses knew that his voice counted most of all. They hurried Christ into his presence to learn his directions.

How could Jesus escape a cross when he had to deal

with a man like Annas? The clever church politician usually forces the prophetic-minded individual to suffer some kind of martyrdom. He may simply see that he never gets a chance. He may oppose everything he does, or he may shrewdly sidetrack the man who dares to speak what he knows is true. Annas could not stop there! He went further, because his hate of anything like a prophet was deep-seated in his soul.

Annas had lived off unthinking people. He had reaped the harvest of many offices. A man like that would not have much chance to continue in this course if the ideas and principles of Jesus prevailed. It is not to be wondered that he urged the people to shout, "Away with this man!" In the deepest sense imaginable, it was either "away with this man" or "away with Annas"—and all he stood for.

II

From Annas they took Jesus to Caiaphas, the high priest then in office, the son-in-law of Annas. Here was the actual head of the Jewish church government.

Caiaphas had been appointed by Valerius Gratus, the former procurator of Judea. Then he had been permitted to continue his office by Pilate, who had succeeded Gratus. Caiaphas had held this place of ecclesiastical honor for eighteen years. He was manifestly a man of some ability.

More important than that, as far as retaining his office was concerned, he was an adroit individual. He had not merely listened to Annas. He also knew how to accommodate himself to the ideas and plans of Rome. He had learned how to make friends and win influence, *with the influential*. Caiaphas was clever enough to pay attention to those with authority.

Quite obviously the man was prejudiced. As has been suggested, he was so biased in his judgment that he might well have asked, as did another, "Can any good thing come out of Nazareth?" Unfairness, of course, always accompanies prejudice. Jesus had pointed this out when he told why many people would not come unto him. They had already set the course of their lives in another direction. Prejudice has always had a pronounced tendency to become bitter. Caiaphas was most acrid in his attitude toward what he did not like.

The wise person always seeks to rid his soul of prejudice, even if others have done much to embitter him. James Weldon Johnson once said: "I will not allow one prejudiced person, or one million, or one hundred million, to blight my life. I will not let prejudice, or any of its attendant humiliations and injustices, bear me down to spiritual defeat. My inner life is mine, and I shall defend and maintain its integrity against all the powers of hell!"

For the sake of one's own self, if for no other reason, one needs to be free from mental bias. It warps the soul and destroys one's sense of fairness. It makes it impossible to live with oneself, and still be in good company.

Caiaphas was condemned by the very principle of justice itself. Honesty and goodness always condemn shrewd dishonesty. One of the outstanding scenes in *Pilgrim's Progress* is the trial of Faithful. The jury of Vanity Fair had little difficulty in disposing of this character. They said that as far as they were concerned his case was a closed one. How could it be otherwise when they had already made up their minds?

Said Mr. No-good, "Away with such a fellow from the earth." "Ay," said Mr. Malice, "for I hate the very looks of him."

Then said Mr. Love-lust, "I could never endure him."

"Nor I," said Mr. Live-loose, "for he would always be condemning my way."

This is a perfect picture of what happens again and again when right and wrong meet. The evil

64

person hates the very sight of a good man. Goodness always condemns wickedness. And evil that is condemned by goodness that crosses its path always becomes enraged with anger. It loses its temper. It abandons all control of good judgment.

Further than this, like Annas, Caiaphas could not bear for the crystal purity of Christ to become the standard of the people. That would mean not merely the loss of his job, but the loss of his power. His prestige would be forever gone. He could not stand the idea of losing his influence or his means of livelihood.

Back in the nineteenth century many of the politicians in England said: "Let parsons quarrel about the creeds, so long as they support the police." If the ministers only helped keep order, the political leaders would readily put up with their eccentricities. Many of the preachers, however, became local magistrates as well as spiritual police. One of the inevitable results of this "adjustment" is seen in the weakening of spiritual influence. It happened then. It has occurred frequently since then.

In certain states in our own America one sees numerous advertisements of "marrying parsons." They are perfectly willing to use the church as a means of economic gain. The holiness of this blessed, sacramental relationship, marriage, is completely ignored by them in their eagerness to attract as many couples as they possibly can. If these couples are in a hurry to be tied by some parson, it is all the better for these "licensed" ministers. When the church officials that permit this kind of travesty begin to realize all that is involved, they will repent in sackcloth and ashes.

These commercial-minded ministers work upon the traditional sentiment of many people in America who still want the blessings of the church upon their wedding. Many of these men know nothing of the dignity of the lovely wedding ceremony. They understand even less of its spiritual implications. They are thinking only in terms of how many couples they can persuade to visit them. The name of Christ is only a decoration. The Christian motive and spirit are excluded from consideration.

Caiaphas would understand the subtle and, yet dominant, ideas of these men who seek a position in the church for the sake of the ulterior gain that will come from it. He well knew how to use religion for the sake of power, prestige, and personal profit.

III

Caiaphas, however, did try to suggest that he was

keen in his thinking, that he had an appreciation of
the more serious note of religion. He asserted that it
was expedient for one man to die for the rest of the
nation. He had probably heard some statement of
Jesus quoted which indicated that he expected to face
suffering. Caiaphas was preaching the doctrine of the
"scapegoat." But he did not know what he was saying.
He was not aware of its deeper religious implications.
He was simply trying to salve his own conscience—if
indeed he had one! Possibly he was also suggesting
that he was endowed with the spirit of prophecy, which
was supposed to belong, to some extent, to the descend-
ants of Aaron.

Caiaphas had exercised his political activity inside
the Jewish church, and he wanted to appear conver-
sant with its background. Doubtless he did know much
of its records. But he was far beyond his depth here.
He sounded like he was talking wisely. He was actually expressing a great idea, but his motive was altogether ulterior. He was using religion to crush a man
against whom he was bitterly prejudiced. Like some
other legalists, he was perfectly willing to twist the
law to suit his purpose. The scapegoat idea furnished
him a means of justifying his use of instructed witnesses, and may have eased his mind for conducting the

"trial" during the night. This made the court illegal, according to the Jewish code, which forbade any legal business being conducted after sunset.

Caiaphas, however, was running true to type. As has been pointed out by biblical students, some ulterior motive had dominated most of his activities. One has written of how we can damn a fellow-man with an epigram. That is precisely what Caiaphas was doing when he seemed to appear so scholarly.

Fear and fury had such complete charge of his soul that he was scarcely aware of what he was saying. But he knew what he wanted done, and he was bending every possible effort toward its accomplishment. Caiaphas may not have understood Scripture, but he understood his own desires!

Clever politician as he was, he insisted upon following the course of expediency. This is the way most shrewd church manipulators of policy deal with whatever arises inside the organization, or elsewhere. They know how to exercise the most unusual kind of care when it seems to be the discreet thing to do. They have the welfare of the institution at heart, so they say.

They have a habit of pointing out that it is not the time for some strong resolution to be passed—such as is being presented. They insist they are in favor of condemning evil uncompromisingly. They are in harmony with the proposed action. But it is not quite the time to take such a positive step. It is not expedient at the moment. They do not bluntly say they are thinking in terms of place, of political power, or of ecclesiastical prestige; but these are obviously their controlling motives as they suggest needless delay for dealing with social wrongs.

Caiaphas, however, went further than simply to quote a religious phrase. He insisted that he was interested in things spiritual. In the company of all the chief priests and elders and scribes who were assembled together, it was an excellent time for him to demonstrate. When the counsel sought witness against Jesus so that they could put him to death, they were a bit embarrassed at the lack of evidence. Even the false witnesses they had gathered together had not been properly coached. Their testimony disagreed. It must have been a bit disappointing to those who were so eager to rush Jesus to his death. There were some, however, who arose to give this disconcerting testimony: "We heard him say, I will destroy this temple that is made with hands, and within three days I will build another made without hands."

Caiaphas stood up in the midst of this assembly. He

asked Jesus, "Answerest thou nothing? What is it which these witness against thee?" Jesus held his peace. There was no need of answering Caiaphas. He would not have understood. Furthermore, he was not really interested in the matters that concerned the very soul of Jesus.

Again Caiaphas turned to him, asking, "Art thou the Christ, the Son of the Blessed?" Jesus answered: "I am: and ye shall see the Son of man sitting on the right hand of power, and coming in the clouds of heaven."

"Caiaphas rent his clothes and cried out, What need we any further witnesses? Ye have heard the blasphemy: what think ye? And they all condemned him to be guilty of death."

It is dangerous to try to evaluate any man's sincerity. It is too deep a matter to judge lightly. Who can say there was no sincerity in this protest of Caiaphas? There may have been. But it is also quite obvious that he was using the gesture for all it was worth. It "went over" with the crowd.

He had achieved his purpose. He had worked up the fury of the mob. The whole assembly readily asserted that Jesus was guilty of death. Some began to spit on him, others to buffet him. Some sarcastically cried out, "Prophesy!" as they struck him with the palms of their hands. It was a severe experience for Jesus, one that must have cut his soul to the quick. His entire conduct is a demonstration of greatness— the nobility of a Divine Character.

The painter Briton Riviere represented Daniel as an old man down in the pit, gazing in front of him with a sort of awe and reverence. It was as though the beasts that were cowering before him only suggested another manifestation of the power of God. Here is an old story used by a famous painter. But the truth is eternal. *To be one with God is to have his power.* It is the dynamic of love.

Jesus knew that the Heavenly Father was with him. He was not afraid of Annas, or Caiaphas, or all the mob who had gathered together. Rather he loved them all —and that made his agony of soul all the more intense.

IV

There was no way for Jesus to escape suffering. What chance did he have in the presence of a man like Caiaphas? The judge had already abandoned justice. He had no idea of listening to all the evidence in fairness. His mind was already made up like that of another. Caiaphas was simply going through the forms of justice when the case of Jesus was presented. The church trial of Jesus was mere mockery.

Any trial is just this when those in authority are shrewd, clever politicians, such as were Annas and Caiaphas. The only possibility for a prisoner, facing a group like that, was death. The Cross was simply inevitable.

HEROD, WHO BARTERED HIS SOUL FOR PLEASURE

And when Herod saw Jesus, he was exceeding glad: for he was desirous to see him of a long season, because he had heard many things of him; and he hoped to have seen some miracle done by him.

—Luke 23:8

THE ENEMIES OF JESUS WERE DETERMINED THAT HE should die. That is why they hurried him away from Caiaphas to Pilate. Only the Roman government could pass the sentence of death.

But Pilate does not keep this strange prisoner long. He hears that he is from Galilee. He anxiously inquires: "Art thou a Galilean?" A bright idea seizes him. Herod is in the city at this very moment. He has come for the Passover. It is not an unusual legal procedure to transfer a prisoner from the official in whose territory he has been arrested to another in whose province he has been born, or in whose he has held his residence.

Pilate was greatly relieved. He was eager to shift the responsibility. Certainly, at the least, he wanted someone to share it with him.

Of course, as has been suggested, it is possible that

73

what Pilate wanted was advice. Festus once brought Paul before Agrippa in order that he might be advised by one who understood something of the customs of the Jewish group to which Paul belonged. But the latter part of the official trial indicates quite positively that Pilate was eager to be rid of his responsibility.

At any rate, Jesus was now being sent from one official to another. He had first been carried to Annas, the clever church politician. Then they had ushered him into the presence of Caiaphas, who was also a shrewd manipulator of ecclesiastical machinery. From Caiaphas they had carried Jesus to Pilate, and now Pilate was sending him to Herod. And he was not yet through with this rude treatment by men who ignored, or did not care to consider, the deeper issues in his trial.

I

Who was this Herod? We need to know him in order to understand his attitude toward Jesus. There had been a king called Herod the Great. He was the ruler who slew the babies at the time of Jesus' birth. Insanely jealous of his power, he was fearful of even a baby whom certain wise men prophesied would be a King. This Herod had ruled over the whole country, under the authority of Rome. At his death the dominion had been divided among his sons. Judea had been given to Archelaus. But this province was soon taken away and administered by the Roman government, through certain procurators. Pilate was one of these. Galilee and Peraea were given to Antipas. This was the Herod to whom Jesus was being carried. He had manifestly inherited much of his father's nature. He was desirous of power, and jealous of others who might weaken his hold or thwart his ambitious schemes.

But his moral downfall soon came. There was little fibre of character in his personality. Though he was married to the daughter of Aretas, Emir of Arabia, he entered into an intrigue with Herodias, the wife of his brother Philip. The Arabian princess did not wait for a divorce, but indignantly fled to her father. Herodias left her husband to come and live with Herod.

There are many people today related to these two, by immorality! Without openly announcing they are going to do so, hosts who are socially ambitious are abandoning righteousness and purity. Insisting upon self-expression, many of them are giving vent to the lowest kind of sexual passion. That is why they rebel so violently against any individual, or any church, that holds high the standard of sexual decency.

Most students feel that Herodias was a stronger personality than Herod. Certainly she was inordinately ambitious and furiously headstrong. She was determined to squeeze everything she could out of life for herself. It was as though an evil spirit had clothed itself in flesh and come to live with Herod. Her influence over him was so great, Herod scarcely realized himself how powerful it was.

He, however, had some characteristics that recommended him. They should not be overlooked. Students of his reign have pointed out that he was interested in architecture. Tiberias, which he built, reminded the people of his wider interests in life.

Furthermore, Herod had some noble aspirations. Who does not? Even after he had lapsed morally, so that he gave up the appearance of being virtuous, he continued some show of religion. In an especial way did John the Baptist appeal to him. He invited the rugged prophet to his palace, where he listened eagerly to the ringing message of this daring proclaimer of righteousness. That is, he listened until John said: "It is not lawful for thee to have her."

This struck him where he was most vulnerable. Herod could not stand this kind of preaching. It was all right for a man to speak boldly, to proclaim truth

76

uncompromisingly, so long as it did not affect *him* and *his* life! Or, at least, so long as it did not concern what he was most intent on doing, or the way in which he was most eager to live. When he himself was accused of moral failure, Herod reacted just as most of us do. He did not like it! He violently rebelled. He threw John in prison. He had to punish the man. He was taking too many liberties. He was forgetting who ruled the people. Even though he was imprisoned, however, John still disturbed Herod. His message cut deep lines in his soul.

Herodias was extremely agitated. She both feared and hated this man. She feared him because of his daring; she hated him because he rebuked her sin. He was making life miserable for her. She plotted his downfall. She planned it with the shrewdness of one who was as wise as a serpent and as wicked as the devil.

Very likely Herod did not understand all that was going on. He was not keenly sensitive enough to suspect her evil plans. Quite frequently people prejudice us against other individuals when we do not understand how much bitterness is in their hearts. Sometimes it is a woman who whispers words of acrid malice in our hearts, but whispers them with such a

77

smile that we are taken unaware. We are caught off guard. Sometimes, it is one who poses as an intimate friend. The effect is always damaging; sometimes it is disastrous.

II

Then there came that tragic night of unrestrained lust when Salome danced before the drunken company of officials. She stirred their passions to a greater rage as they reveled with their women. Salome was the daughter of Herodias and Philip. She was a young girl with physical charm and social cleverness. Like most of the others in the company on this lustful night, Herod was intoxicated. But the skill and beauty of Salome affected him mentally and physically far more than did his wine. He was drunk with her charm. He lost his head. All his life he had been a devotee of physical pleasure. In this drunken riot he made a foolish vow—to be more accurate, the vow of a fool. He said he would give Salome whatever she wanted, even to half of his kingdom.

When Salome demanded the head of John the Baptist on a waiter, Herod suddenly came to his senses. It was as though one had dashed ice water in his face. It was a rude awakening. He realized he had spoken rashly. He keenly regretted what he had said. But he did not regret it deeply enough. He was not genuinely repentant. He foolishly felt he had to stick to the pledge of a drunken babbler that was made to a nude dancing girl. Libertine as he was, then living in the shame of open sin, he nevertheless professed to have some sense of honor. He would keep his word. As a result, John was beheaded.

But Herod could never forget John. The dissevered head of the bold proclaimer of righteousness was probably in his imagination much of the time. He could see those lips move. He could hear what they said. The words of this rugged prophet were constantly coming to his mind. He remembered the uncompromising integrity and moral boldness of the man. *John the Baptist loved righteousness as passionately as Herod loved beautiful women. Herod could not forget a man like that!*

Herod knew that he had sinned. Even rationalizing could not free him from this consciousness. Indeed, he had sinned so much that he could little understand the tragic nature of vice. For, as Martineau once pointed out, "Sin is the only thing in the universe of which it may truly be said that the more you practise it, the less you know its nature."

Obviously Herod was not disturbed enough to turn

away from his lust. He had deliberately chosen sensuality. He was unwilling to humble himself enough to pass through the wicket gate of repentance into life. But he was still troubled about all that had occurred.

III

This explains why Herod was so eager to see Jesus. Jesus reminded him of John. There was an uncompromising spirit about this Strange Man, this Devotee of righteousness whom some called the Messiah. There was a fibre of character about Jesus that reminded Herod of one whom he had earlier admired and then foolishly executed. He actually thought he might be John come to life again.

Furthermore he was excited about what Jesus had been doing. He had heard that he was able to work miracles. Herod's curiosity was aroused. And it was of an inordinate nature. He could hardly wait to see Jesus. To be sure, he was putting the Master on the level of a dancer, or of a public singer, or of an Oriental juggler; but he did not even stop to think about what he was doing. He was too eager to have his curiosity satisfied. He felt greatly complimented, too, that a high Roman official would send a prisoner to him. It made him prouder than ever.

Here Jesus is before him. *But the presence of Jesus does not change the character of the man.* The bent of his will was too firmly set. He had spun his own fate. Drunken Rip Van Winkle, in Jefferson's play, easily excused himself for every lapse, every indulgence. He would say: "I won't count this time!" Well, he might not count it, but his nerve-cells, with scientific accuracy, were registering every drink.

Discerning observers could see Herod's lust even in his countenance. For, as Henry Drummond says, "God gives to each of us our features, but we make our own faces." Gilbert Stuart, the famous portrait painter of George Washington, made a study of facial expressions. Once when he looked at Talleyrand, the French statesman, who was visiting America, he remarked: "If that man is not a scoundrel God does not write a legible hand." God does, indeed, write a legible hand. The face of Herod Antipas told much about the man of which he himself was not aware.

But he kept on talking foolishly, just as he had done in the past. He was not a religious man. Here, therefore, was a way of life far beyond his experience. He did not understand it. It was out of his range. Yet even when he faced Jesus, he kept talking, though he knew practically nothing about religion. Everything he said disclosed the shallowness of his mind.

Herod was like a great many people today. They enjoy discussing religion objectively, or academically. They have a certain amount of curiosity about it. They speak their opinions quite freely, because their ideas do not amount to much. They express themselves without any hesitation, because their opinions are only opinions—and not convictions. Many a forum on religion is only an occasion for airing the views of those who participate. Few who *debate* on the different phases of Christianity are eager to follow its truth with the passion of knights who have sworn allegiance to Christ.

Herod's curiosity was excited like that of a child. He wanted to see Jesus perform a few of his miracles. Trifler that he was, he evidently looked upon them as the tricks of a magician. That is what they were, as far as he was concerned. The multitudes had believed in their genuineness, but Herod was sure that Jesus was only another Oriental magician. Tradition tells us that there were pictures of grapes on the walls of the room in which Herod talked to Jesus. The king requested that Jesus change these to real grapes. It is only a story out of the distant past which is not based on sufficient evidence to warrant its historicity. But the supposed request is entirely harmonious with the character of Herod. It was not beyond him to ask for such to be done. Why not? Was he not the ruler? Were not his pleasures the law of the land?

Herod is the only individual, according to the biblical records, to whom Jesus referred with a stinging phrase. He had called a *group* "whited sepulchres," but he called *Herod* "that fox." As has been suggested, anything that Jesus might say to this crafty and sensuous ruler would be like throwing pearls before swine. What good would another appeal to this man do? What would it accomplish? John the Baptist had given enough directions for any man who wanted to follow the right. This prophet of righteousness had told Herod specifically what to do. For his testimony, John got his head chopped off.

IV

There is the semblance of a trial that proceeds. It really is not a trial. What takes place is not worthy of this term. Jesus refuses even to offer testimony. What good would it have done? Why should anyone talk to Herod? The Master may have recalled an ancient proverb of the Jews: "Answer not a fool according to his folly." The person who would stoop to do that would become a fool. He would have to make himself one in order to be understood.

Herod simply was not a deep man. He might have been, but he had refused to cultivate the element of potential worth in his nature. His soul had withered away because of his lust for physical pleasure. He had fed his physical appetite and starved his heart. Herod reached the place that he simply did not understand things that were spiritual. He did not want to be troubled with any serious thinking. It was too much bother.

There were people like that in John Wesley's day. Bishop Berkeley wrote in *Siris*: "Whatever the world thinks, he who hath not much meditated upon God, the human mind, and the *summum bonum,* may possibly make a thriving earthworm, but will most indubitably make a sorry patriot and a sorry statesman." Carlyle's verdict on the same era was: "Stomach well alive, soul extinct." Mark Pattison writes: "The historian of moral and religious progress . . . . is under necessity of depicting the same period as one of decay of religion, licentiousness of morals, public corruption, profaneness of language—'a day of rebuke and blasphemy.' "

84

The Cross was inevitable when there were people like Herod who were responsible for the trial of Jesus. How could Jesus escape the Cross, when he had to face such a man as his judge? As a matter of fact, such a person as Herod could not understand Jesus at all. For one to understand Christ requires a genuine desire to know the truth and a holy dedication to follow the truth, "like a sinking star beyond the utmost bounds of human thought."

v

Some people have thought that Jesus should have seized this opportunity to try to convert Herod. Either they do not understand Herod, or they do not appreciate Jesus. It is likely that those who think this understand *neither one of them*. One must have a sense of right, or at least one must be willing for one's devotion to honor to be awakened, if Christ is to be able to make any appeal. Herod was virtually past spiritual feeling. He seems once to have had a conscience, but he had refused to heed it for so long that the inner voice could scarcely be heard.

Moral leprosy had practically anesthetized his soul. A story found in the chronicles of William of Tyre tells how it was discovered that Baldwin, son of Amory, the

King of Jerusalem, was a leper. One day, when the future king was playing with his comrades, the hands and arms of all the children were scratched. The other boys cried out in pain, but Baldwin made no complaint. When he was questioned, he affirmed that he felt no pain whatsoever from the scratches. "His arm and hand had gone to sleep, and even when his tutor bit him, he did not feel the bite."

Dr. Victor Heiser says he has often seen a lighted cigarette burning into the fingers of a leper without his being at all aware of it. "Even the odor of burning flesh did not attract his attention, because the sense of smell was also gone." Herod may not have quite reached this state morally, but he was not far from it.

What could Jesus himself do with a man who was so deeply in love with sin that he was not willing even to listen to the voice of righteousness? Certainly Jesus loved sinners. He always sought to help them. No one ever fell so low that Jesus was not eager to help him. The woman who came in off the street where she had been meeting men who were willing to buy her body was happily received by Jesus. He forgave her graciously. His pity surpasses all our understanding. But, you see, that woman was repentant. She bathed the feet of Jesus with her tears. Her soul was exceedingly sorrowful. She was ready to forsake the past.

There was a man crucified with Jesus who had sinned grievously. But he had not sinned so much that Jesus was unwilling to help him. When that man repented and sincerely sought the aid of Jesus, he heard the voice of the Master saying: "Today thou shalt be with me in Paradise." Christ will forgive the worst of sinners, if he will accept forgiveness. There was no one the Master would not help, provided the individual earnestly yearned for his divine pardon. *But even Christ cannot do anything for the person who refuses his aid.*

Jesus would have dealt kindly with Herod, even though he was the murderer of John the Baptist, if there had been one salty tear of repentance on his cheek. But that tear did not even form in the eye of Herod. There was only idle curiosity and the supercilious smile of one foolish enough to think he understood the deepest Mind and greatest Soul this world has ever known. If we could forget the tragedy of it, it would be ridiculous.

There was no word of forgiveness then, because Herod had refused to obey the voice of righteousness in the years that had gone before, and because he was still unrepentant. He was lacking in spiritual sensitiveness. He could not feel the great challenge of Holiness in his heart. *When a man refuses to heed the Voice of God, he is sure to lose his way!*

VI

This was the kind of man before whom Jesus was being tried. How could he escape a cross when such people as Herod dealt with him? The Cross was inevitable for Jesus, because his judge did not have enough spiritual understanding to appreciate the very principles which were involved in the trial. All that Herod said only disclosed a corrupt soul.

Jesus, who said, "Only the pure in heart see God," was standing before a moral reprobate. Jesus the Righteous was standing before Herod the compromiser. Jesus the Holy was being tried by the sordid, pleasure-mad Herod. How could he escape the Cross?

So Christ cannot escape the Cross today. Think of the people who, like Herod, have lost their souls in order to have one physical thrill after another. Although they do not even understand the Master, they lightly and flippantly render their verdict. They insist that lust is worth more than love. They are so eager for new forms of excitement that they do not have time to consider the deepest matters of righteousness, goodness, and truth.

Hosts of people who are dealing with Jesus know no more of spirituality than did Herod. Yet they unhesitatingly pass their verdict upon the Master. They send him to the Cross. *So long as there are people like Herod, there must be a Cross for Christ!*

PILATE, WHO TRIED TO SHIRK HIS RESPONSIBILITY

And when they had bound him, they led him away, and delivered him to Pontius Pilate the governor.

—MATTHEW 27:2

PILATE'S EFFORT TO BE RID OF JESUS PROVED FUTILE. When the accusers of Jesus first brought him to Pilate, the Roman governor sent them to Herod. Following his experience with this pleasure-mad ruler, Jesus was brought back to Pilate. Doubtless the Roman governor wished he had remained in Caesarea, his official residence. It was the Passover season, however, and as usual he had come to Jerusalem at this time.

Caiaphas comes at the head of the group who are condemning Jesus. He and his cohorts are so eager to speed up the execution of this so-called Messiah that they are impatient with every delay. The Roman governor, however, insists upon understanding the situation. Simple justice demands this, and Rome is recognized for the fairness of her legal courts. "What accusation bring ye against this man?" asks Pilate. The religious leaders have accused Jesus of blasphemy, but now before Pilate they use another argument. They realize there must be another approach if they win the aid of this official. They therefore assert that Jesus has been perverting the nation. They accuse him of setting himself up as a king.

They are clever enough not to suggest their real reason for wanting Jesus killed. They do not now refer to his religious ideas. They prefer using *ad hominem* argument. They know the good sense of appealing to Pilate where he will be most vulnerable. Had they simply talked about their conflict with Jesus' religious teachings, Pilate would not have taken the matter seriously. We readily recall the well-known incident enacted before Gallio: "And when Paul was now about to open his mouth, Gallio said unto the Jews, If it were a matter of wrong or wicked lewdness, O ye Jews, reason would that I should bear with you: But if it be a question of words and names, and of your law, look ye to it; for I will be no judge of such matters. And he drave them from the judgment seat."

Though the mob was becoming unruly, Pilate made an effort to save this Strange Prisoner. He takes Jesus inside. The two of them are face to face. It is a dramatic incident that no one will ever be able satisfactorily to paint or adequately to describe. Pilate was looking in the face of the most kingly Man he had ever seen. Undoubtedly he was convinced of his innocence. Why then did he treat him as he did?

I

If we understand the conflicting forces which were sweeping across the mind and soul of Pilate, we must recall at least something of the background of his life. In A.D. 26 Pilate succeeded Valerius Gratus in the administration of Judea. It is likely that he entered his office with a desire for peace. This was decidedly preferable for any ruler. His attitude, however, was one that provoked opposition. He portrayed the Roman's feeling of haughty superiority over those who were not Romans. He looked down upon these foreign subjects whom he was expected to keep in order. He did not possess the tact or the patience of some provincial governors. Indeed, there are some students who assert that Pilate's ability did not measure up to some of the former officials of Palestine.

At times he seems to have been openly hostile to the Jews. He did not seek to be conciliatory. He was too stubborn to choose the course of wise expediency. The eagles and the image of the emperor on the military standards were especially obnoxious to the Jews. They constituted a special kind of insult to the Jews, who had for long years been so violently opposed to idolatry in any form. When Pilate refused to order his soldiers to remove these insignia, a committee called upon him. For several days they offered their protests. Instead of being moved by their appeal, however, and trying to appease them, the governor became even more provoked. Their request only deepened his prejudice against these inferior colonists who dared tell him how to run his affairs. He refused to yield in any way until he realized certain regrettable consequences might follow and he, of course, would be held responsible. It was not his regard for the people or their desires that caused him to answer their appeal.

Some time later Pilate set up gilded shields in Herod's palace. The Jews considered these another form of idolatry. They seemed to suggest the worship of the emperor. The people were enraged again. They felt they were being insulted and their religion was being scorned. Again they petitioned Pilate. When he did not immediately answer their request, they threatened to take their appeal to the emperor. Pilate was at his wit's end. He did not want to yield. It would apparently indicate weakness on his part. On the other hand, he did not want to lose his office. There are some who think it was his fear of impeachment that plagued him. At any rate when the Jews carried their appeal to Tiberius, he ordered Pilate to remove these shields. The governor had been humiliated. He could never forget it. It was in the background of his mind all the time the trial of Jesus was taking place. He was none too eager to help these Jews. Yet, ironical as it was, again he was being forced into a decision that went against the grain of his mind and will.

Pilate undoubtedly preferred justice when it did not interfere with his own deepest desires. But it is also obvious that he was lacking in the necessary strength for a really great official. How much of the arrogance of the harsher type of Roman officer he had cultivated is a matter of dispute. He likely did have confidence in the sword as the most effective means by which one could get things accomplished. Furthermore, Pilate had learned how to see things in their "practical" light.

There were many good deeds that Pilate had to his credit. The ancient records tell us that he had given Jerusalem, for the first time, a water supply. It is an indication that he had some sense of obligation to the provincials over whom he ruled. He was not without his good points.

94

His love for power may have occasioned some of the regrettable acts of his administration. There is a reference in the thirteenth chapter of Luke to one of his brutal deeds. "There were present at that season some that told him of the Galileans, whose blood Pilate had mingled with their sacrifices." Here we get a glimpse of the harsher side of the man's character. How pronounced this was it is not easy to say. Certainly, however, we know that things material were quite real to Pilate. He was a believer in force. The army was a symbol of real power, and he loved authority.

With even this brief background, it is at least easier to understand some of the things Pilate said, and why he acted as he did during the trial of Jesus. He was afraid of these accusers of Jesus, though he would have been the last person to admit this fact. He feared what they might do. His official position was too precarious already, and here were people who knew how to remind him that it was necessary to keep Caesar's friendship.

II

Yet there can be no doubt that Pilate wanted to save Jesus from the threatening execution.

He hated the whole business of the trial. It created

95

a revulsion in his mind. He felt here was some minor infringement of Jewish law that scarcely deserved his attention. The proconsuls were always eager to steer clear of all local affairs of the Jews. They were especially eager to avoid dealing with ecclesiastical matters. In the first place, they realized they did not thoroughly understand them, even though they had a contempt for all these strange religions in the colonies of Rome. Further than this, Pilate, like other colonial rulers, simply did not care to meddle in any minor affairs of the people over whom he had been set as an official, unless it became imperatively necessary.

On the whole, the New Testament writers are not overly critical of Rome's representative. Those who have left the earliest records were apparently impressed with the idea that Pilate did not want to condemn Jesus. It is interesting to note that the Passion Play at Oberammergau emphasizes this idea in the scene which presents the Roman official having the trial forced upon him. The village players have so stressed this that one who witnesses the drama feels that the governor was far more friendly to Jesus than he was to his accusers.

In spite of his evident condescension, Pilate seems to be fairly courteous to Jesus as he seeks to learn just what his business is. It is probable, to be sure, that he was a bit cynical as he asked for a definition of truth. As one of our essayists has suggested, he may not have waited for an answer. He likely thought it was impossible to give an adequate answer to that perplexing question.

There is an incident, to which Professor Luccock refers, that sticks like a burr in the mind. It is contained in a report of an interview of Van Paassen with Marshal Lyautey, the French colonial administrator and empire builder of North Africa. A rainstorm made possible a chance meeting on a library porch in Paris. Mr. Van Paassen had the opportunity to ask the French proconsul his opinion of Pontius Pilate as a colonial administrator. Marshal Lyautey had a great deal of scorn for Pilate's lax government in allowing Jesus' teaching to spread so far.

"What would you have done, had you been in Pilate's place?" Van Paassen asked the African war lord and governor. "I would have settled the whole matter early and easily by putting Jesus in front of a firing squad when he was up north in Galilee," said Lyautey.

Pilate was at least better than Lyautey!

III

But there is a responsibility that history will not permit Pilate to avoid. Nor can those of us who now read the records lift this obligation from Pilate's shoulders. *He did have Jesus on his hands.* Furthermore, he was the Roman official charged with a duty he could not transfer to some other person. *He simply lacked the courage to do the thing that he knew he ought to do.* Even when one insists that Pilate probably did what he thought was the clever thing, he still had this unusual warning from his wife: "Have thou nothing to do with this just man, for I have suffered many things in a dream because of him."

"What is it you are really standing for?" Pilate asked Jesus. "What is your real business? Why are you willing to endure so much?" The answer Jesus gave was so plain that it should have been easy for the Roman official to understand—if he had only listened. "I am come to bear witness of the truth." As has been suggested, probably these words would move us more deeply if they had been translated, as well they might be: "I am come to be a martyr to the truth." Then Pilate asks, "What is truth?" He was a hard-bitten man of the world. He belonged to a group who were more interested in cleverness and power than they were in the solid facts of life. In the words of another, his comment might have been like this: "My dear sir, when you are as old as I am, you will be less willing to die for an idea. When you know people as well as I know them, you will agree that they don't want to be made unusually good. They want to eat and drink and enjoy their light loves. They want a fairly good time; thereafter they will jump the life to come."

Of course, Pilate tried to evade his duty. There is the bowl of water in which he symbolically bathed his hands clean of the whole affair. The act only served to emphasize his official duty. A bowl of water big enough to hold the ocean would not be sufficient to wash away the responsibility of Pilate—nor of you and of me!

As a Roman official he had been trained in the principles of justice. He well knew that justice was not being done. He may have thought that he was acting discreetly, that he was using his head. He certainly was not using his conscience. He was trying to drown out the voice of right in his soul.

Yet it seems he did try to do the right thing. This is the strange inconsistency of the man. There is no doubt but that Pilate was a stern and harsh governor. He likely thought it was his duty to be rigid in his regulations. He knew that he was responsible to the emperor for a group of people who had been considered difficult subjects. He failed because he had done many wrong things in the past. A past weakness which had conditioned so many of his acts made it extremely difficult for him to do the right thing at the moment he needed most of all to reach the right decision. He had shaped his character, and his character necessarily made his decision what it was. If he had been more honest, just, and brave all through his life, there would have been a different scene enacted before him on that notable day. He had a glorious chance to write a page in the history of the world that would provoke gratitude on the part of Christians for all the centuries that followed. But he missed his high hour. He thought he was trying an ordinary Jewish citizen—a strange one to be sure, but one among thousands. He was really being tried by Christ. *Pilate was so anxious to save his skin, as well as his face, that he lost his soul.*

IV

But what can we say about ourselves, we who live in this twentieth century? We, too, have power. We have influence. We have the duty and the inescapable responsibility of making decisions. To be sure, most of ours do not involve so many people as did those of Pilate. Here, however, is the matter of supreme importance: *they all deal with the same Man who faced Pilate.*

How often we, too, lack nerve! We may have thought out something so well that we are sure of what we ought to do, but then we let circumstances make our decisions for us. We are afraid. We do not admit that we are, but we let certain conditions keep us from doing the right. It may be fear of what others will say. Frequently it is fear of what others may do. But it costs us terrifically. After such failures, we cannot stare our own selves in the face. Like Pilate, we too say Jesus is innocent, but we go on to condemn him to death.

We may wash our hands, or say that we are washing our hands of the whole matter, *but we cannot do that any more than Pilate could. We have our responsibilitiy just as did he.* It takes courage to do the right. It requires dauntless daring to do what is Christian. No one of us can summon this by his own resources. It requires the power of God. Many of us are not merely afraid; we have never accepted the grace of

Christ by means of which we are able to do the things we know we ought to do.

It may startle some of us to read that in the same statement he declares Jesus a righteous and innocent man Pilate is willing to condemn him to death. But many of us do the same thing. We only make some weak affirmation of the greatness of the Master. We give him our lip service. We are sure that we too are innocent of the blood of the just man, but our influence goes against him. It may be that we want to keep our jobs as Pilate wanted to keep his.

Most of us know that many things are wrong today, but we do not want to take a positive stand against them. We may lose the friendship of certain people whose good will we covet. We do not like to be laughed at. We do not like to be called narrow, or puritanical, or revolutionary.

We know that righteousness exalteth the nation, and that social injustice and needless unemployment are reproaches to any people. But we try to shift our responsibility of citizenship. We feel that the broken laws of God and man cannot be laid at our door, at the very time we refuse to do anything about building up public sentiment of a virile and strong nature for a Christian social order.

Some people sell their souls for a seat in the senate—or perchance it is only a seat in the state legislature. Then they make public speeches about the need of national morals and political ethics. It does not mean much to those who have discerning minds. They see what has occurred.

Recall that scene when Lady Macbeth was endeavoring to wash the blood spots from her hands. As she wrings her hands, she is heard to say: "Out, damned spot! Out, I say! .... Here's the smell of the blood still: all the perfumes of Arabia will not sweeten this little hand. Oh, oh, oh!"

The perfumes of Arabia would not sweeten her hand. The washbowl of Pilate would not cleanse his hands. Our declarations of our own innocence, and our acknowledgments of justice and fairness will not relieve us either. It is not that easy to get rid of our guilt.

There are some interesting traditions concerning Pilate. One account says that he was thrown into the Tiber, where even though he was weighted with lead his body would not sink. There is another tradition which asserts that he was thrown into a lake in Switzerland where every year on the anniversary of the trial his body reappears on the surface and washes its guilty hands in useless regret.

They are but traditions, but they powerfully suggest how the world has recognized the impossibility of Pilate to be free from his guilt. There are reminders for us too that it is impossible for us to be free from our guilt.

We are responsible unless we do all in our power both to expose evil and save the evildoers. This is fundamental Christianity. No one can evade this obligation. Furthermore, we have had centuries in which to learn more about the importance of Christ. We know what he represents. We know for what he stands. We know that when we deny him we are denying the highest, the truest, the best the world has ever known. Woe unto those who, living in the twentieth century, try to evade the responsibility which belongs to all who face Jesus Christ!

WHY THE CROSS, FOR GOD?

He that hath seen me hath seen the Father.

—John 14:9

CHRISTIANS HAVE ALWAYS FELT THERE WAS A VITAL RELA-
tionship of the most intimate nature between Jesus
and God. Many people have tried completely to
humanize Jesus, but again and again they have been
forced to face his divine beauty and to consider his
heavenly character. All Christians are sure that they
know more about God since Jesus lived than ever it
was possible to learn before. This is a fact of momen-
tous importance. Of course, no one has ever pointed
out scientifically the precise relationship of God to
Jesus. There have been various theories, but none has
ever been quite satisfactory. The really significant
fact is that men have felt so much of the Godlike in
Christ that they have tried in unnumbered ways to
explain the vital relationship between the two.

Nowhere is it more important to understand the
intimacy between God and Christ than in this matter

of the Cross. If one is able to catch a vision of the nature of God in the suffering of Jesus on Calvary, one has gone far toward understanding Christianity.

I

When Jesus declared, "He that hath seen me hath seen the Father," he gave new direction to the entire course of religion. This fact means that Jesus gives us a picture of God's very character.

Jesus went on to point out that God must care deeply for us since he cares for things so inferior to us—the lilies, the birds, and even the grass of the field. God values us more highly than he does all material things. "You are worth so much," declared Jesus, "that if you gain all the world and lose your real self, you have lost everything. This is the way God values you."

When Jesus looked with compassion on the multitude, he was showing us how God himself looked upon humanity. If we could have seen the face of the Master, we would have caught a glimpse of the heart of God.

So too God knew the agony of Jesus' broken heart, the indescribable suffering of his lacerated soul. God was on the Cross all the time Jesus suffered. He had to be. He felt everything Jesus felt. He was pained with his pain. He suffered with his wounds.

The Heavenly Father felt the pains and experienced the agony of Jesus because of his relationship to his Son. Dr. Leslie Church tells of a friend to whose life came a great tragedy. His only child, a little girl, became blind because of gross carelessness. For a moment this father's world crashed. Then suddenly he crept into the shelter of the Heavenly Father's love. He remembered that God's Son was slain upon a Cross. He gathered himself together by means of the new strength this fact gave him. The rest of his life was given to a lovely ministry of devotion to help others. Men and women listened to his message and gained fresh courage. He attracted little children. At the end of a long day he would go home to his blind child. Together they cultivated happiness beyond words. There was a sacred bond which held them together. It was because first they had been bound to God by the knowledge of his compassion.

He that spared not his own Son did not spare himself! God did not merely endorse what Jesus did. He was with him. Jesus is the portrayal of the Divine Father, even on the Cross. For God was in Christ reconciling the world—you and me—to himself. When we survey the wondrous Cross, we witness the visible

symbol of a spiritual love which can never be adequately expressed in words.

"All things have been delivered to me: and no man
knoweth the Son save the Father; neither doth any
know the Father, save the Son, and he to whom the
Son will reveal him."

Jesus was plainly talking of an intimate relationship
that the Cross finally demonstrated in a dramatic and
realistic manner.

This certain hope of Christianity saves our universe
from being an insane asylum. It gives meaning and
significance to human existence.

If, however, we accept this faith, we see that man can
hurt God—that we who sin do pain him beyond
description. Love alone can measure the suffering
inflicted on the one who loves. Our God cares! He is
no Absolute, who holds himself aloof from all our
affairs, who cannot be touched by our infirmities or
wrongdoing. He suffers because of all we do that is
wrong.

This is not the hurt pride which some parents feel,
nor is it that weakness that superficially talks of another's having hurt one's feelings. This is the pain of
God whose love is so great that he must suffer untold
agony when we reject his heart's devotion.

II

The love of Christ is the love of God. God suffered just as much as did Christ. He does now. He must if what Jesus said is true: "He that hath seen me hath seen the Father." That is why Studdert-Kennedy once declared that the hardest part to play in the world is surely God's part.

Many people had been crucified before Jesus. Men had hung stoically on crosses before. It was not the physical suffering which made Jesus cry out in agony. His most intense suffering was of the heart and soul. It was the fact that he cared for us so much and we violently rejected every gift of his heart that made this Cross so heavy.

Most of us have felt that Christ had a love for humanity surpassing human understanding. Where did this love of Christ originate? How did it come to be? Where did Jesus learn it—so that he could live it? There is only one answer: "He who has seen me has seen the Father." The Deity was expressing himself in Christ so perfectly that no statement is adequate unless one definitely asserts that Jesus was divine as well as human.

III

When men became so wicked they made a cross, God had to suffer! He suffers with all his children.

The Cross was inevitable for God because he made men free to choose either the highest or the lowest, the best or the worst; and men chose the worst. That is a simple statement. But what indescribable tragedy it suggests!

The age-old story of Enoch walking with God is a dramatic suggestion of what God wants all of us to experience. But we can refuse the friendship of God. We can reject his love. We can send God to the Cross! His love for us is so great that his suffering is inevitable if we refuse the best he can give—even himself.

God knew the risk involved when he made us with the prerogative of deciding what we would do. But unless we had the ability to say "No" to God, we would have been no better than the animals which are guided by their physical instincts. Or, perchance, we would have been like mechanical toys which one winds up and then watches run down. But we were made free to choose, so that we could become like God, and enjoy his love forever. We can decide to reject, or to respond to, the Divine appeal. *God will not force us to do right, even though he himself is Right, and longs for us to choose that for our lives. If we are ever good, we must have the chance to be evil.*

This means that we can spoil our own lives and crush the hopes and longings of our Heavenly Father. We can so constantly choose wrong that it warps our lives.

This is how and why the Cross itself was originally invented. Men became so filled with vengeance they wanted others to suffer worse pain than they had ever felt. We read how two men in a Carthaginian glen ran their enemy down. They bound him hand and foot and then sat beside him, considering in their brutal hatred what they should next do with him. Mere killing was too good for him. That would let him off too easily. They must kill their hated enemy slowly. At the same time, they wanted to inflict intense torment and extreme indignity so that others might never think of his death without nausea and horror. This is how they came to invent the vile instrument of impalement. That is what the cross was meant to be, and became.

Years went by, and then Rome in her moral decadence took over from Carthage this means of inflicting horrible suffering. The government, however, reserved it for aliens and for the worst criminals. Certainly as an invention the cross comes out of the very slums of the human heart. The terror-inspiring truth is that it is a revelation of what man at his worst is capable of doing. It shows what we can become in hate and cruelty.

God had foreseen this possibility. When he made us with the capacity to cultivate spite and lust for murder, until we even created a cross—or the modern equivalent, in the horrors of war—he immediately chose to risk the possibility of our nailing him to that Cross.

When men became hateful and murderous enough to invent the cross, they stabbed the soul of God himself.

IV

But God has a dual vision. He sees us as we are, and as we could be, with his help. He is always dreaming of—and planning for—our future, for all we can become. That is why he suffers when we fail him. We may not be hurt with the moral lapse of others. We may even discuss their moral failures, with a bit of relish, because of our morbid curiosity. *But God cannot do that. His heart is cut to the quick every time one of us fails, morally, ethically, or spiritually.* Otherwise the term "Father" would have no real meaning.

Even when we fail him, he keeps on urging us to come to the higher life.

"Daughter, thy purity is ever before me," says God.

"Son, the honor of thy life is ever before me," says the Heavenly Father.

The man you meant to be in your best hour is always in God's mind and heart. God's heart must be lacerated, cut with deep gashes, caused by our sins, when we fail our best selves—and him.

Olive Shreiner once said she would hate to be God. One can understand that. For Divine Love to have to face the miseries and heartbreaks which afflict men and women and children around the world is to feel pain such as no mere human can know.

Georgia Harkness writes:

> "I listen to the agony of God—
>   I who am fed,
>   Who never yet went hungry for a day.
>   I see the dead—
>   The children starved for lack of bread—
>   I see and try to pray.
>
> "I listen to the agony of God—
>   I who am warm,
>   Who never yet have lacked a sheltering home.

In dull alarm
The dispossessed of hut and farm
   Aimless and 'transient' roam.

"I listen to the agony of God—
   I who am strong,
      With health, and love, and laughter in my soul.
   I see a throng
   Of stunted children reared in wrong
      And wish to make them whole.

"I listen to the agony of God—
   But know full well
      That not until I share their bitter cry—
   Earth's pain and hell—
   Can God within my spirit dwell
      To bring his kingdom nigh." [1]

The greater one's capacity to be pained, the more one suffers. Some animals suffer very little, especially those on the lower levels. The delicate structure of man's body makes him suffer more, even physically. His keen mind and intricate nervous system compel him to feel much more intensely than a mere animal ever could. Think how greatly God must suffer, because of his spiritual sensitivity!

A true mother is pained when her child deliberately

---

[1] "The Agony of God," from *Radical Religion*. Used by permission of Miss Harkness.

lies when he is old enough to understand what he is doing. The mother suffers when she thinks of the years ahead and of what this habit may later mean to the child, and to his life. So God our Father suffers when we sin because he can see our sin in the light of the long, long years ahead.

v

In every picture of Christ's suffering we see God's suffering. When Christ cried, "I thirst," he was expressing the thirst of God.

Without water, life itself becomes unbearable. When one is scorched by the blazing sun and driven to desperation by the sense of great suffering, the tortures of thirst become indescribable. Coleridge attempted to portray a bit of this in "The Ancient Mariner." The stricken men are on the becalmed ship in midocean. The blistering sun only intensifies their agonies. Beneath the torrid heat, unrelieved by rain, or even fog, the pitch is slowly bubbling in the seams of the deck. The plaintive cries of those tortured men are echoed in the words of the sole survivor:

> "Water, water, everywhere,
>   And all the boards did shrink;
> Water, water, everywhere,
>   Nor any drop to drink."

Now God was thirsting like that—for the souls of men. Our capacity to love measures quite accurately our capacity to suffer. That explains why the suffering of God was—and is—so intense. His love is so great!

Briants, the sculptor, was so poor he could not even afford fuel for his studio. The night he finished the model of his statuette of Mercury, the weather was very cold. He was fearful lest the damp clay freeze. He had bestowed too much labor and love on this precious figure to see it ruined. He took off his own coat and wrapped the clay model in it.

The next morning they found Briants dead from cold. The statuette remained perfect and unharmed. It is now in the Paris Gallery of Fine Arts. God loves us even more than that!

The most difficult-to-understand word spoken by Jesus on the Cross is, "My God, my God, why hast thou forsaken me?" Rambach, whose volume *Meditations on the Sufferings of Christ* once fed the piety of thousands of Christians, asserts that when Jesus uttered that agonizing cry, God was dealing with him not as a loving and merciful Father with his child, but as an offended and righteous Judge with an evildoer. "The heavenly Father now regards his Son as the greatest sinner to be found beneath the sun, and discharges on him the whole weight of his wrath." Even to use such language, however, means that one is venturing beyond one's depth. As has been suggested, the comment of Bengel is much to be preferred. He writes: "In this fourth word from the cross our Saviour is not only saying that he has been delivered up into the hands of men, but that he has suffered at the hands of God something unutterable." Quite obviously there is in this word of Jesus something altogether unutterable! What makes it more profound, however, is the fact—fundamental to all genuine Christianity—that Christ's life, his suffering and death—all is a revelation of the divine nature. It must be for Christianity to be true! God could desert Christ only as he deserted himself!

Whatever else we may say about the fourth word of Jesus on the Cross, "My God, why hast thou forsaken me?" we know that God was still suffering. He had not freed himself from pain. He had not deserted Jesus, so that he could breathe easily a brief moment while Jesus went on suffering. If that were true, when Jesus declared, "He that hath seen me hath seen the Father," he did not mean quite all he said. For then Jesus would have been more than God—yes, better than God. *No! The most Godlike thing Christ ever did was to go to the Cross!*

VI

But why all this suffering, you ask? Why should God suffer, even if we have sinned? There is only one answer: To redeem you and me. Salvation is still possible only by means of Love that pays the full price, that goes all the way, that takes the sins of the sinner on his own heart.

If one says God ought just to forgive us without suffering, one discloses a woeful ignorance concerning the nature of forgiveness. Forgiveness is the most expensive gift one can ever bestow. We don't "just forgive"—not anyone who really forgives. He who can forgive easily loves little.

Certainly the mother forgives the daughter who has broken her heart. She eagerly and sincerely forgives. Yes, but the scars caused by her sorrow and suffering remain. There are deep lines of pain in her soul.

Suppose one ruined the life of your child—in a far more realistic sense than this phrase once suggested— so that your child would never have the future for which you dreamed and planned. You could never

118

describe how deep the wound had gone—even if you did forgive the transgressor.

There are those who refer to the story of the prodigal, and suggest that God could do what this father did— forgive and joyfully receive the returning prodigal. Well, God *is* the Hero of that story. But he did not carelessly pardon the guilt of the prodigal. Anguish was in his heart all through the years that son was away, living as though he had no Father. And though he forgave his boy, the soul of the Father was cut to the quick.

God has a plan for us, and when we do not follow this plan, we suffer and God suffers. When we wander away into sin, he must be deeply pained.

Why the Cross, for God? The Cross was necessary, because evil and God came together. *When sin runs athwart Holy Love, that always makes a Cross.*

Redemption is both deep and high. It reaches from highest heaven to our deepest needs, though it has to descend to hell. That's why it costs so terrifically.

When we survey the wondrous Cross, we do get a vision of God. Calvary is the measure of God's love. And, as strange at it seems, the Cross which was created *by evil men* has become *God's way of saving us from evil.*

WHY THE CROSS?

Here is the greatest symbol of God's power we have. *God goes to the Cross to win us from wickedness, because he loves us to the death, because he is willing to pay any price to save us unto life!*

WHY THE CROSS—FOR YOU AND ME?

And whosoever doth not bear his cross, and come after me,
cannot be my disciple.

—Luke 14:27

"If any man come to me, and hate not his father,
and mother, and wife, and children, and brethren, and
sisters, yea, and his own life also, he cannot be my
disciple." These are strong words. If we were not so
familiar with them, we might think they were an over-
statement of what Jesus originally said. We might
believe that some scribe had edited the early manu-
script. But we know Jesus too well to deny that he
spoke these words. They are in harmony with his life.
To be sure, the language is emphatic, with character-
istic Oriental vividness. But Jesus' ringing challenge
still thrills and dares us: "Whosoever doth not bear his
cross, and come after me, cannot be my disciple."

I

Of course no one can possibly appreciate this exhorta-
tion of Jesus unless he knows, at least to some extent,
why the Cross was necessary for Jesus, and indeed for

the Deity himself. If, however, God could not escape the Cross—if in Christ we have a dramatic manifestation of the suffering, the pain, the agony of God—then we begin to understand the deeper meaning of Jesus' words. There are still circumstances and conditions akin to those which originally produced the Cross. The conditions constantly surround us. Is the disciple above his Lord, or the servant above his Master? If not, the Cross must be necessary for you and me!

The scholars have given various reasons for the necessity of Christ's Cross. Some of these have been quite crude, materialistic, and unsatisfactory. But every effort which has been made has had some value. It has at least served to emphasize the inescapable necessity of the Cross.

Some have said that there was a *ransom* paid. Others have insisted that a *vicarious sacrifice* was necessary, that Christ became a *substitute* for us, one which sufficed to answer the demands of a Holy God. With almost unanimity of emphasis, the scholars have insisted that Christ was a *Saviour* who died for man. Most of the terms which the teachers of theology have used have been inadequate and unsatisfactory. This one, Saviour, has had meaning across the centuries. All these terms, however, have been the result of efforts to explain one of religion's greatest mysteries. Instead of assuming a superior attitude toward the biblical students, whose interpretations have necessarily been only partial, we would do well to accept the fundamental fact they emphasize, namely, *the eternal importance of the Cross.*

Every serious attempt to interpret the Cross has suggested at least this truth: that here God in Christ was doing something for man which man could not do for himself. If we can grasp that central fact, then we have gone far enough to understand much of this experience of Christ on the Cross. *God in Christ was doing something for you and me that we could not do for ourselves.*

The second fact which we need to face, with frankness and honesty, is this: *so long as one does not see any need of the Cross, one will not be benefited by the Cross.* The fact that we do not realize this truth explains much of the spiritual weakness of the church today. The Christ of the Cross can help only those who so gratefully recognize their need of him that they seek his salvation.

This is a very simple statement to make, but the truth is not simple. It is profound. Furthermore, it has been so frequently demonstrated that no one dare ignore it, except to the peril of his soul. There are people who try to ignore the Cross. They think it is outside the need of the intellectuals. Thus do they intend complimenting themselves in a most subtle way.

There are many churchmen, moreover, who think of religion only in terms of organizations, or of business efficiency, or of helpful efforts in the realm of charity. They think theology is not theirs to understand. They feel there is too much mysticism about the Cross. They declare they are not mystical-minded. Thus do they talk superficially, and thus do they miss life! *They miss the Saviour!* All that has made the church of eternal significance and everlasting worth is lost, as far as they are concerned. *No one will ever know the deepest power of the Cross in his personal experience unless, first of all, he realizes that he needs the Cross.*

A more than interesting incident occurred during the gold rush of 1849. A United States frigate was anchored in the harbor of San Francisco. The crew had heard wonderful stories of the riches in the nearby goldfields. They were led to believe it would be no trouble to have them. It was almost like picking up gold. Some of these sailors could not resist the temptation to join the crowd, filled with lust for gold. Even if murder was necessary, they felt it was worth it. The boat's crew killed and threw overboard a young ensign. Then they set off in haste for the goldfields. But they did not all escape. Two were caught. They were brought back to their ship, tried by court martial, and sentenced to death.

The ship's captain came ashore and made arrangements for a minister to see these sailors before they paid the penalty of death for their crime. The minister who came to see the two condemned men pointed out the source of spiritual aid. On the morning of the execution he went on board early. He carried with him the vessels with which he was to celebrate the Holy Communion. He also brought the brass cross from the altar of his church. The officers of the ship knelt side by side with the condemned men to receive the bread and wine. How dramatic that scene! There were the two nooses dangling in the air, waiting to be used. On the communion table was the brass cross, the emblem of hope to those two men, convicted of their crime.

Once the cross was only a gibbet for criminals. See what Jesus has done for it! Because he died on it, for our redemption, it is the symbol of our salvation.

What a vivid scene that story presents, so suggestive in its power that we dare not ignore it, except to the peril of our own souls. The danger which many people face, however, is that they will think the brass crucifix suggested a Cross that was necessary for these criminals, and then will go no further in their thinking. It did suggest the only hope those murderers had, but it also symbolizes a Cross which is necessary for you and for me.

Who does not need the Cross of Christ? Who is too good to feel that its benefits are not for him? He who considers himself above or beyond the Cross will remain outside the pale of its grace. In so classifying himself, he becomes Pharisaical; and Jesus insisted that harlots and publicans go into the Kingdom ahead of the Pharisees. It is because harlots and publicans feel the need of the Saviour who hangs on the Cross.

"God forbid that I should glory save in the Cross of our Lord Jesus Christ!" That is the way the greatest Christian of the first century, certainly outside the circle of eleven disciples, felt about this matter.

A recent English writer has related a story about a chaplain in the Great War who, as he rode past a ruined church in the battle area, was greatly surprised to hear the sound of music. He got off his motorcycle to investigate. There was not much left of the church. It had been smashed to bits. The seats were "little better than matchwood." In a corner was the only thing left unharmed. It was the little organ. There at the console sat a British soldier. He was a young lad who, the day before, had gone through the hell of battle. He had found his way to the church, where he discovered the little organ. He laid his fingers on the keys. He began to play. Then he forgot everything save things in the past. He was playing the old familiar hymns and tunes of home. There rang through the church a bit of Mendelssohn's "Hear My Prayer." Then he played "Oh for the Wings of a Dove." Then he changed to the hymn they sang on the sinking of the *Titanic*, "Nearer, my God, to thee, e'en though it be a Cross that raiseth me." He played again. This time it was the great hymn, "Rock of ages, cleft for me, let me hide myself in thee." Once more the young soldier played, this time singing the words of the hymn, "In the Cross of Christ I glory, tow'ring o'er the wrecks of time." As Dr. J. D. Jones has said, that lad, even amid the havoc and desolation and danger of war, was seeking his center of life. He found it in the Cross and the love that Cross reveals.

We may not fully understand the Cross. Who can? But we can realize our need and thus turn to him who is the Saviour of all who sincerely come to him. He offers his salvation. He can and will deliver and redeem us from all that is sordid, mean, little. When we begin to understand ourselves, we know, too, that the heart is "desperately wicked." "Who can understand his errors? Cleanse thou me from secret faults."

It does not matter who we are, there are two things that need to be said so clearly we can never forget them: The Cross is necessary for all of us. If, however, we feel no need of the Cross, we will not be saved by the Christ of the Cross.

II

This statement of Jesus, however—"Whosoever doth not bear his cross, and come after me, cannot be my disciple"—involves something else. Not merely do we need to know that the Cross is necessary for ourselves; we need to take it up in the spirit that Jesus took up the Cross. To be sure, Christ died on Calvary in a way in which we can never die. There is something eternally unique about the Cross of Christ. But, this is also true: *any individual who experiences the benefits of the Cross will want to take up the Cross in order to carry it himself.* This is at the center of the teachings of Jesus. It is at the heart of all he had to say. Nobody knows the benefits of the Cross unless he knows the

128

glory of bearing it himself, for the sake of others who have not even felt any need of it.

In failing to see this truth, and stress it, the church has lost much of its power. The people who have been able to lead others to the Cross have themselves borne the sorrows and sins of others.

Consider C. F. Andrews, recently deceased, who went around the world telling people how to find God, how to be quiet in his presence, and how to sense spiritual reality. Sometime ago he was speaking in New York City before a group of young business men. They turned to him and said: "Don't tell us about India, tell us how to pray." So well had he learned the high art of praying that many asked him to teach them how to pray. So he went about, teaching others in a plain, simple way the art of communing with God. Why? C. F. Andrews had learned how to bear the Cross. To India he went, to do just this. He felt the pains of India. He carried upon his own heart the cares and burdens of people whom he came to know. In the spirit of the Christ, he shouldered the problems and perplexities of his fellows. He was always trying to relieve the afflictions of the oppressed. That is why he knew how to pray!

To the extent that we receive the benefits of the

Cross of Christianity—to just that extent—do we ourselves take the Cross, so that others can gain these same benefits and blessings.

Walt Whitman did not write the best poetry America has produced. There are many of his verses which some of us do not like. But there is one thing many people have forgotten about Whitman, namely, that he did put himself in the place of humanity, that he bore the sufferings and sorrows of others. In one of his poems he says that he does not simply feel the burden of the one who suffers. He suffers too. He does not have to ask the wounded man how he feels. He becomes the wounded person. He writes that he walks handcuffed to jail along with the mutineer. He knows the agony of the cholera patient. He gasps with him at his last breath. "My face is ash-colored—my sinews gnarl—away from me people retreat." Agonies, he declared, had become one of the changes of his garments. Walt Whitman had learned how to bear the pain of others.

In 1877 Richard Green, the English historian, was deeply troubled by the policy of his nation. He wrote in a letter: "I love England dearly. But I love her too well to wish her triumph if she fights against human right and human freedom. Pitt longed for her defeat in America, but it killed him when it came. I can understand that double feeling now." Here we clearly see how love is the measure of our deepest suffering.

Here is something the Christian Church must recover if it ever receives the benefits of the Cross, or demonstrates its significance and its saving power.

This is the substance of the Cross: *It is to accept responsibility for something or for someone for which or for whom we have no responsibility, legally speaking.* That is what the Cross was for Jesus. That is what it will be for us.

As H. R. L. Sheppard has insisted, if any individual thinks he has anything to contribute to human welfare without a share of suffering, he is "living in a fool's paradise, which is no paradise at all." Calvary has taught us this.

Sometimes, when one asks some people to help others to be more loyal to religion, they say, "It looks like people could do what is right by themselves." Well, suppose Jesus had assumed that attitude? Suppose he had said: "Let every man look after himself." What of humanity? What of us? There would have been no Cross, no Saviour!

There is a story of the great Russian writer Andreev, which, as Professor Luccock has well said, deserves to be included in the service book of every church in Christendom. The story tells how the events of the crucifixion were seen through the eyes of a character named Ben-Tovit. On the fateful day of the crucifixion he was able to grasp clearly only one thing, namely, that he was suffering from a toothache. He caught fleeting glimpses of the tragic progress along the Via Dolorosa. Every now and then he had a flash of a figure on a hill, outlined against the sky. But that was all he saw. He had the toothache. He was worried with his own trouble. He was preoccupied with his own physical suffering.

The story is almost too vivid. It might well be included in the devotional literature of our church. Think of your being in Jerusalem that day, as Ben-Tovit, seeing Jesus walk along the Via Dolorosa with the Cross, going on out to Calvary. But you have the toothache! Your tooth hurts while Jesus is being crucified. You have practically no idea of what is happening. You only get a glimpse of this Man as they are carrying him out to Golgotha.

It is this kind of preoccupation with less important matters that is robbing the church of its real power today. We are withdrawing ourselves from where we can see the Cross, refusing to be pained by it, until we

132

have lost the magnetic force, the drawing power, which Calvary alone can give. There will be no real power for our church until there are more people in it who are saved by the Cross, more people who are willing to carry the Cross, more people who are willing to accept the responsibility of redemption for others for whom they have no legal responsibility. That is what the Cross means!

In the year 1688 that great Christian, John Bunyan, was preaching his farewell sermon. He was in a room in Whitechapel. Frail and ill as he was, he was thinking of others' spiritual health. Ardent devotion for God and for men burned in his heart. "Dost thou see a soul," he pleaded, "that has the image of God in him? Love him. Love him. Say to thyself, *'This man and I must go to heaven together some day.'*" That is how one feels when the spirit of Christ possesses one. To be sure, one will see more meaning in those words today than did the people of the seventeenth century, but the experience is fundamental.

Jesus tells us to love our neighbors as ourselves. Surely that means we should share with them a large part of the care and interest we naturally feel for ourselves and our welfare. Jesus goes on to tell us, in the inimitable story of the Good Samaritan, that *anyone who needs us is to be counted as our neighbour*.

There is no power for any church, no matter what else it may do, until that church learns how to pray with the agony of men's present needs and spiritual welfare on its own heart, until the hearts of Christians are pained as Jesus' heart was pained. This is the only justification for any church that carries as its symbol the Cross of Jesus Christ. This is the only force that will save us, our church, or humanity. It is the only experience that will give power to bring men into the Kingdom of God.

If we say that we are willing to take a Cross only when we are guilty, then it becomes only a means of punishing us for our sins. That is not the Christian Cross! The Cross before Jesus was a way of making men pay for their crimes, but *it was not that for Jesus. For Jesus it was a means of taking the sins of others upon himself*. That is what the Cross becomes for us when we are saved by the Christ of the Cross. To take upon ourselves the sorrows and sufferings of other people, for which legally or otherwise we have no responsibility—that is real Christianity. That is what made Jesus Godlike. That is what will give us the power of Heaven. There is no other way to gain

134

it. Of course it is a most exacting experience, for *the Christian Cross cannot be streamlined.*

Rabindranath Tagore, sensitive soul whose love for afflicted mankind deeply moves one, was so torn in his heart by the suffering of Abyssinia that he sent messages to the press and to the emperor. He was pained by the callous greed which led people to indulge in hypocritical practices on those who were weaker. His love of peace and his antipathy toward war made his pain all the more intense. At the same time, he lamented the state of his own country and carried the burden of his own people's sorrows.

He who can look out upon our torn and distraught world today without pain is certainly not akin to Christ!

Albert Schweitzer says he feels the sufferings of people to whom he is ministering, that their troubles crush his soul. He is one of the truly great modern Christians, and this is what has made him great. If even a small group in any church could experience this, something would happen that would send them through the community as a mighty saving force, throbbing with love. It would be the spirit of Christ taking hold again, saving us from our littleness, from our selfishness, and from everything that is unlike the Master, unto the power of the Cross.

An English writer has given us a story concerning one who went to Bethnal Green to serve the needy there. He was an old Oxford blue, and a man of intellectual brilliance. When the first World War came he was over fifty. Most of the workers in his group were naturally taken from this Oxford settlement, in East London. But he shouldered the burdens. Then his eyesight gave out. The doctors said one eye would have to be removed. With hardly a word he went to the hospital on Monday morning, and was back at work Tuesday afternoon. An extreme case? Yes, but it demonstrates what one can still do for the unfortunates of the world if the sacrificial spirit of Christ has captured one's heart.

All of us have probably seen a few people come to express agony in their faces because they were trying to shoulder the Cross. It is not possible to gain the greatest religious power in any other way.

In his letter to the Colossians, Paul writes one of the most startling statements he ever penned: "I Paul . . . . now rejoice in my suffering for you, and fill up that which is behind of the afflictions of Christ." We too must "fill up" again the sufferings of Jesus. Here Paul

136

is writing something that searches our very souls. It startles us. *We must "fill up" the sufferings of Christ, which he himself did not complete.*

We must take up that Cross again. There is one for each of us, but it is accepted only by those who are saved by it. We are set free by the Cross only when we carry the Cross ourselves. We are saved *by* it first, to be sure; but to be saved *by* it is also to be saved *unto a spirit that makes us want to bear the Cross.* To be redeemed is to be made, at least to some extent, into the likeness of Christ. It is to be saved to the character of Jesus, to the throbbing heart of Jesus.

Quite obviously it is much more difficult to shoulder the Cross than it is to recite a creed about the Cross, but it is the former experience in which Jesus is most vitally interested. Or why did he say: "If you would be my disciple, take up your cross and follow me"?

Let us ask ourselves whether we love all of Jesus? Are we devoted to all of Christ? We love him, of course, when he ministers unto us, when he comforts us. Do we love him on the Cross? Do we love his pain, his agony, his Cross? Do we love Jesus when he takes upon his own soul the burdens of humanity? Do we love him for bearing the sins of mankind? Then we will take up that Cross too!

Do we love this Christ, who cannot be satisfied unless he does something for us that we do not deserve to have him do, but which he yearns to do because he is Godlike? Are we willing to take into our hearts the Christ who loved even Judas, those who plaited the crown of thorns, and those who drove the nails through his hands and feet? Truly to love this Master is to follow him through that same kind of experience. There is a very sacred and spiritual absolution which every genuine Christian brings his fellows. After all, *Christianity has one real weapon: sacrificial love that knows how to suffer.*

There is only one way to know that the Cross will set men free again. It is to welcome the Divine Saviour of the Cross into our own souls, so that, through you and me, this Christ may live again as a Redeemer!